Language Learners in the English Classroom

Language Learners in the English Classroom

Douglas Fisher
San Diego State University

Carol Rothenberg
San Diego Unified School District, California

Nancy Frey
San Diego State University

Foreword by David Freeman

National Council of Teachers of English
1111 W. Kenyon Road, Urbana, Illinois 61801-1096

Manuscript Editor: Jane M. Curran
Staff Editor: Bonny Graham
Cover Design: Frank P. Cucciarre, Blink Concept & Design, Inc.
Interior Design: Doug Burnett

NCTE Stock Number: 27049

Library of Congress Cataloging-in-Publication Data

Fisher, Douglas, 1965–
Language learners in the English classroom / Douglas Fisher, Carol Rothenberg, Nancy Frey.
p. cm.
Includes bibliographical references and index.
ISBN 978-0-8141-2704-9 ((pbk))
1. English language—Study and teaching—Foreign speakers. I. Rothenberg, Carol. II. Frey, Nancy, 1959– III. National Council of Teachers of English. IV. Title.
PE1128.A2.F543 2007
428.007—dc22

2007022649

Contents

Foreword

It was the best of times. It was the worst of times." The opening lines from Dickens's *A Tale of Two Cities* could describe almost any classroom in the United States. In the past, in many parts of the country, most students entered neighborhood schools with similar backgrounds and life experiences. Now the student population is much more diverse. Creative teachers have capitalized on this diversity and broadened the horizons of all their students. When a class reads a novel about Asia, eastern Europe, Africa, or Latin America, there are often students in the class from one of these areas who can provide insights into the history and culture of the region and enrich the discussion of the novel. Similarly, student writing often reflects an incredible variety of experiences. Student diversity brings new perspectives to the classroom and expands educational opportunities. In many ways, increased student diversity makes this the best of times.

But for many teachers, this is also the worst of times. They feel burdened by the constant requirements to benchmark and test their students. Teachers often complain they are so busy testing that there is no time to teach. In addition, some schools have adopted programs and materials that limit teacher choice. In these schools, teachers may feel more like technicians following scripted directions than like true professionals who can choose resources that meet the needs of their students.

When teachers are expected to bring every student to a high level of academic achievement quickly, diversity becomes a problem. Rather than drawing on the varied experiences of students from different linguistic and cultural backgrounds, teachers often focus on the students' limited English proficiency. If some of their students don't speak English well, and if these students have limited background knowledge in academic content areas, teachers face an almost insurmountable obstacle in raising their academic achievement to expected levels in a short time. The challenge is greatest in secondary schools where the academic load is heaviest.

Schools usually hire ESL specialists to work with students whose English is extremely limited. At the secondary level, most English language learners (ELLs) are placed in one or two periods of ESL classes each day. However, mainstream teachers, and especially English teachers, still have the major responsibility for teaching English language learners. *Language Learners in the English Classroom* provides theoretically sound, practical ideas that can help English teachers work effectively with the ELLs in their own classes and, at the same time, provide the help their colleagues in other subject areas need. Following the ideas the authors present, secondary English teachers can become leaders in shaping the education of the English language learners at their school.

The National Clearinghouse for English Language Acquisition & Language Instruction Educational Programs reports that during the ten-year span from the 1994–95 school year to the 2004–05 school year, the general K–12 population grew from 47.75 to 49.0 million students, an increase of 2.6 percent. During that same period, the population of limited English proficient students grew from 3.2 to 5.0 million students, an increase of over 60 percent. Many states reported a rise in their ELL population of more than 200 percent. Areas of the country with very few English language learners in the past suddenly have large numbers of second language students.

Across the country, one of every ten students is classified as limited English proficient. Much of this increase has come at the secondary level. The growth rate of immigrants is significantly higher in secondary schools, a rise of 72 percent compared with 39 percent at the elementary level. As a result, secondary teachers across the country need a clear understanding of how best to work with ELLs.

The authors begin by reviewing the demographic changes that have occurred in schools. Next, they explain some differences among the ELL population. Some students come with high literacy in their native language. Although these students need support in learning English and the culture of American schools, the knowledge they have acquired in their first language transfers to reading and writing in English. This first group of students succeeds academically at high rates. However, the other two groups the authors identify struggle more with school in English, and many drop out. They face the double challenge of learning English and learning *in* English.

Many new immigrants arrive with limited primary language literacy. Some come from areas like Somalia, where war has disrupted daily life. Others come from rural areas where schooling is provided only on an intermittent basis. Students with low literacy in their primary language face a much greater challenge. They may need basic literacy skills, and yet they are expected to read literature and content texts in a new language at the same level as their native-English-speaking classmates.

Some students begin school speaking a language other than English, but by the time they reach the secondary level, their English proficiency approaches that of their classmates. However, many students born in the United States who speak a language other than English at home do not reach grade-level standards of reading and writing in English, even after many years in U.S. schools. In addition, many native English speakers also lack the academic language needed for school success.

Fisher, Rothenberg, and Frey explain these important differences among English learners. Then they list the challenges these students face and outline the instruction they need. The authors draw on an array of research on teaching second language students to identify the key strategies teachers can use to help all their students succeed. As they note, "There is an amazing amount of consistency across these reports." All of the research shows that teachers matter. Good practices can accelerate learning. The research clearly points to specific strategies teachers can use. Literacy is complex, however, and skills are not effectively taught in isolation. Instead, teachers should offer purposeful instruction using appropriate materials.

Drawing on the research, and on their work in a large high school with many ELLs, the authors present a four-step model for teaching English language learners that includes focus lessons, guided instruction, collaborative learning, and independent reading and writing. These four steps provide a gradual release of responsibility. In the beginning, teachers offer a great deal of support through the focus lessons. Carefully scaffolded instruction allows ELLs to engage in the lesson. Gradually, the teacher shifts the responsibility for learning to the students during guided instruction and collaborative learning activities. Eventually, ELLs can complete a task independently. This model offers the support ELLs require to develop the skills and knowledge they need to succeed in school.

The heart of *Language Learners in the English Classroom* consists of the four chapters that follow this introduction of the model. Chapter 3 focuses on vocabulary. This chapter contains many practical ideas for helping students develop the academic vocabulary they need to complete reading and writing assignments in the different content areas. In this and the following chapters, the authors review the relevant research and then explain the specific practices they have implemented. It is this clear explanation of the strategies they have used that distinguishes this book and makes it such a valuable resource.

In Chapter 4, the authors turn to grammar instruction. While traditional grammar is not useful, all students need to develop the conventions of English to communicate effectively. Beginners need to understand the difference between the syntax of a question, "Is it blue?" and that of a statement, "It is blue." More advanced students need to read increasingly sophisticated structures. Chapter 5 deals with fluency, which, as the authors explain, is much more than speed. At the secondary level, students must be able to read and write with facility and with a focus on comprehension. Chapter 6 focuses specifically on comprehension strategies. The authors include suggestions English teachers can use in their own classes as well as ways they can work with colleagues to help them teach their students how to read texts in science, social studies, and math.

Each of these chapters shows how to organize using the four-step approach introduced earlier with suggestions for focus lessons, guided instruction, collaborative learning, and independent reading and writing. Although each chapter concentrates on one area—vocabulary, grammar, fluency, or comprehension—Fisher, Rothenberg, and Frey remind readers that all the skill areas should be carefully integrated. The final chapter shows how teachers can put it all together to make their classrooms a place for language learning.

Language Learners in the English Classroom is a book that reflects the present realities of classrooms across the country that are filled with English language learners. Pressures from testing and scripted teaching materials could make some teachers feel that these are the worst of times. But teachers who follow the ideas presented in this book can build on the strengths that their students from diverse backgrounds bring and turn this into the best of times.

David Freeman
University of Texas at Brownsville

1 The English Language Learner: "My Life's Path Is a Circle"

We fled Afghanistan, leaving everything behind as we made our way to Pakistan. The 12-hour trip in the back of a truck took two days and nights. We climbed mountains, crawled through dirt caves, and hid from certain torture and death. With no food and little water, my mother, brother and I reached Pakistan and wandered the streets for days. After many desperate months, my mother got a job that barely paid for our room. Although we went many nights without food, I had no time to focus on how bad my situation was because my priority was to do well in school and learn Urdu. Education had become my refuge and, once again, my joy in life.

While living in Pakistan for 7 years, we faced many challenges and obstacles. I even stopped going to school because it got too hard to keep my grades up and to pay attention in my classes. I started working in order to support my family. Sometimes I used to see students coming from school. Tears fell from my eyes and I used to say to myself how great it feels when you go to school and learn new things everyday. I used to think that I would never return to school or become the person I had dreamed of.

Then, an amazing event changed my life. After an extensive interview and a home visit from a United Nations High Commissioner for Refugees official, my mother, my brother and I were allowed to fly to America. A journey of two nights and three days placed us on American soil, in the city of Boise, Idaho.

The next morning was a true awakening. Slowly, the darkness that had stretched from the night of my father's and brother's deaths began to lighten and I faced each new challenge eagerly. My biggest obstacle was learning English so I worked hard in class, read more than my friends, listened to the news every night, and spoke English every chance I could. I got help from teachers and friends, who became my mentors and role models.

Now I see my life's path as a circle that I began to walk the day I arrived in America, when individuals opened their hearts to me, and opportunities—like open arms—embraced me. I will widen this circle as I reach out to others to make a difference in their lives.

Arian Dyanat

Think of yourself so eager to have an education, but not able to attend school. Imagine living in constant violence, destruction and war where you lose one or more of your beloved family members. Your family is torn apart, running away to survive, and you are only twelve years old. Yes, it is hard to imagine, but I have lived through it all. Members of my family escaped Ethiopia's tyrannical regime, only to face more terror in Kenya as refugees. We never gave up hope to find peace and freedom and, with determination, finally found a new home in the U.S.A. I still carry my past with me; it is impossible to forget, and it has taught me valuable life lessons about positive leadership and the importance of building community. The obstacles I overcame have helped me develop determination and persistence in any challenge I now face.

"The journey of a thousand miles begins with a single step." I keep this quote in my mind as I keep my family in Africa in my heart. And I believe that my mind and heart will continue to guide me, just one individual, to make this world a better place.

Abdurashid Ali

The journeys of these two extraordinary young people, in their own words, can teach us much about what is possible in the face of seemingly insurmountable obstacles. Their journeys can teach us much about ourselves as teachers and as learners in our own journey toward high standards and high achievement for all our students.

This journey begins with two steps—knowing our students and knowing where we are going. Effective English teachers are in a constant cycle of assessing, planning, teaching, and reflecting. We generally begin the school year with a reading assessment along with a baseline writing assignment where our students demonstrate what they know and can do. We have the content standards and curriculum maps to tell us where we are going. And from there, we plan our first unit of study.

For teachers of adolescent English language learners (ELLs), knowing your students and knowing where you are going means all of this and more. Knowing your students, of course, means knowing their reading levels and their skill in writing. It also means knowing about their prior schooling, literacy in their primary language, and the circumstances of their arrival in this country. It means recognizing how the structures of their primary language and the worldview of their culture impact their comprehension, learning, and use of English.

For teachers of adolescent English language learners, knowing where you are going means having a clear definition of what it means to be proficient in a language, as well as knowledge of language, language learning, and language teaching. Let's begin with knowing our students—who are our English language learners?

The Changing Face of Our High Schools

America is a nation of immigrants. Listening to the heated debate on both sides of the immigration issue, you might think that immigration rates are higher than ever before. In truth, the percentage of foreign-born residents today remains below the peak reached during the late 1800s and early 1900s, when 14 percent of our population was born outside the United States (Capps et al., 2005). Absolute numbers, however, of immigrants are at an all-time high and with the exception perhaps of the health care system, nowhere is this influx felt more strongly than in our schools.

Data from the 2000 census provide a vivid picture of the changing demographics of our country. Six states—California, Texas, New York, Florida, Illinois, and New Jersey—account for the large majority of children of immigrants (69 percent of the nation's total). These states appear to be the first stop for many immigrants, but the 1990s saw other states across the nation with exceedingly rapid rates of immigration: 206 percent growth in Nevada, 153 percent in North Carolina, 148 percent in Georgia, and 125 percent in Nebraska (Capps et al., 2005). In many cases, these are states that historically had not experienced a significant impact of English language learners on the network of social and public services before this time.

This acceleration in immigration rates translates to monumental growth in the population of students who are learning English as an additional language. Nationally, the ELL enrollment grew by 65 percent during the ten-year period between the 1993/94 school year and 2003, while the overall K-12 enrollment remained relatively stable, growing a mere 9 percent. During that same period, fourteen states from Oregon to Kansas to the Carolinas saw growth rates of over 200 percent (NCELA, 2005). See Figure 1.1 for enrollment trends.

Interestingly, in that time, the growth rate of children of immigrants in secondary schools has increased at a significantly higher rate than in elementary schools—72 percent in secondary compared with 39 percent in elementary (Capps et al., 2005). For a number of reasons, this increase is of particular concern. Traditionally, our resources have been concentrated at the elementary school level, providing far more support for language and literacy development. Elementary school teachers are generally more prepared to teach literacy and develop language—much of their teacher preparation focuses on these skills. Class sizes are often smaller, and the teacher-student ratio allows teachers to develop close personal relationships with their students—a factor that

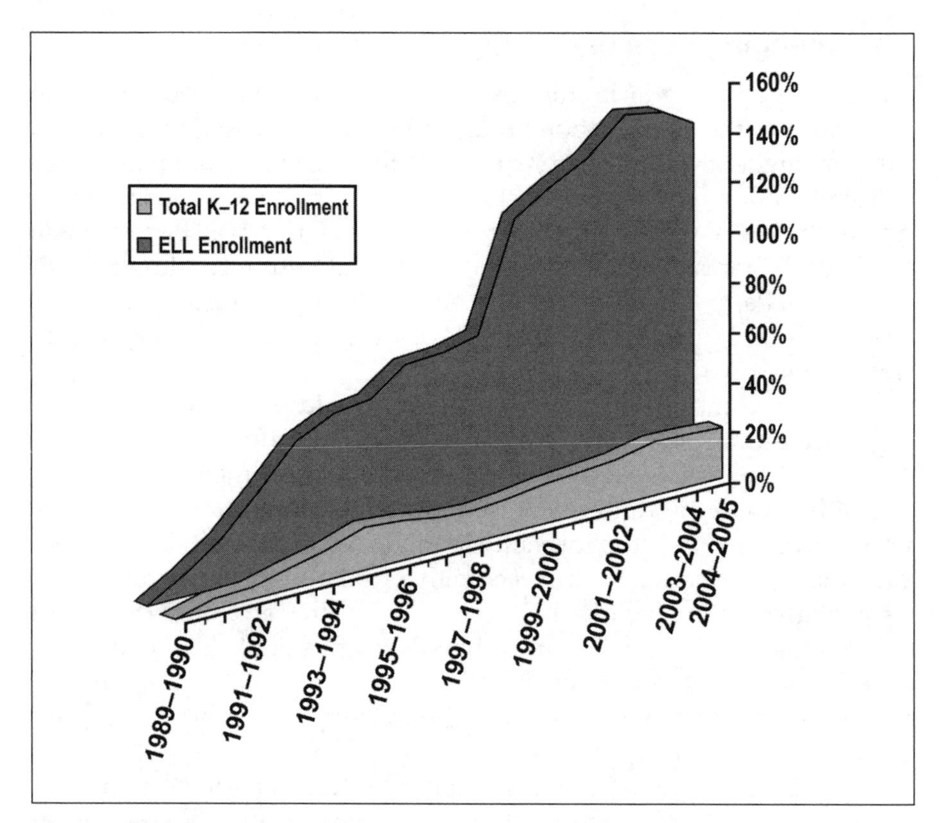

Figure 1.1. Relative growth in ELL and total enrollment in U.S. schools, 1989/90 to 2004/5. *Source*: U.S. Department of Education's survey of the states' limited English proficient students and available educational programs and services, 1991/92 through 2001/2 summary reports. Supplemented by state publications (1998/99 data), enrollment totals from the National Center for Education Statistics, 2004/5 Consolidated State Performance Reports, and data reported by states.

is considered to be one of the most important in current high school reform efforts. An added complication is the gap between the level of an adolescent ELL student's language and the level of language needed to comprehend and produce work that meets middle and high school standards. Finally, the significant majority of our English language learners in secondary schools have been in U.S. schools for several years. Those who have not met the criteria for reclassification (a formal evaluation process that judges the readiness of ELL students to exit from language support services) from English language learner to English proficient by the time they are in secondary school have typically not experienced success in school. They are often disenfranchised, reluctant, and passive learners with fossilized patterns of language and behavior. The dropout rates of foreign-born adolescents make this point painfully clear. An analysis of the 2000 U.S. Census data by the Pew Hispanic Center found that 8 percent of the nation's teenagers were born outside of the United States, yet they account for 25 percent of school dropouts (Fry, 2005). And while we see the same ending for so many of our English language learners, they begin their U.S. education with a wide diversity of backgrounds.

Diversity of Language and Culture

Our English language learners are both foreign- and native-born, with roots around the world. In 2000–2001, states reported over four hundred languages spoken by students identified as ELL (Kindler, 2002). The vast majority—nearly 80 percent—hail from Spanish-speaking countries. Asian languages, such as Vietnamese, Chinese, Korean, and Hmong, are the next most common languages, though none accounts for more than 3 percent of our students (Kindler, 2002).

Diversity of Academic Background

When we label students as English language learners, it is easy to lump them all into one giant category and to describe our 5 million immigrant students simply as being in one stage or another of learning English (NCELA, 2005). And from there, it is easy to place them into a program designed to give them foundational skills in English and hope that, through integration with fluent English-speaking peers, they will experience academic success across the content areas. While all our ELL students share the challenge of learning academic English and gaining access to grade-level curriculum through an unfamiliar language, the reality is that they are a richly diverse group who come to us with different languages, cultures, background experiences, academic skills, and, of course, different needs.

In addition to the individual differences in each of our students, it is helpful to recognize four general categories of adolescent English language learners:

- Recent arrivals with high literacy in the primary language, new to English
- Recent arrivals with low literacy in the primary language, new to English

- U.S. residents approaching native-like proficiency in English
- Long-term U.S. residents with adequate oral English and poor academic literacy skills

Standard English Learners

There is one additional group of students we include in our discussion, a group not technically considered to be English language learners, but a group that teachers across the nation recognize as in need of focused academic language development. These students, born in the United States, are native speakers of English and are often referred to as standard English learners (SELs). These are students "whose home language differs in structure and form from standard academic English" (LAUSD, 2006, para. 5). Major groups include Hawaiian Americans, Mexican Americans, African Americans, and Native Americans. In order to fully understand both instructional and sociocultural issues, it is significant to note that these are "groups who have historically been colonized, conquered or enslaved" (Martin, 2004, p. 5). Standard English learners differ from English language learners in that they understand standard English, while those who are new to the language must learn even basic vocabulary and language structures in order to be able to interact in either social or academic settings. They are similar in that both must learn the vocabulary and structures of academic English in order to be successful in school and beyond. The following strategies have been found to be effective for standard English learners:

- Use culturally relevant literature
- Develop metalinguistic awareness—morphology, vocabulary, syntax, phonology
- Expand use of academic vocabulary
- Use a compare/contrast additive approach to teaching language
- Build on learning styles and strengths that students bring from their home culture (Martin, 2004, p. 15)

Instructional Challenges

Within each of these categories—ELL and SEL—we could easily create a variety of subcategories, but for the purposes of this discussion we will generalize the different challenges each group faces in achieving academic literacy in English.

Recent arrivals who have high levels of literacy in their primary language, along with grade-level achievement in school, are likely to move rapidly through the stages of English language development. The understanding they already possess about how language works, about making meaning from text, and their knowledge and use of strategies to facilitate learning, allows them to focus on the primary task of attaching a new lexicon and linguistic structure to familiar skills and ideas. This is not to say that all they need is vocabulary and grammar; indeed, language proficiency is much more complex than labels and forms. We can, however, generally expect that these students will face fewer challenges as they progress toward proficiency in English.

Other immigrant students arrive with limited formal schooling, resulting in limited literacy in their native language and a lack of foundational academic knowledge. These students often must learn basic concepts of reading and writing at the same time as they are learning a new language and a new way of life. Specialized district- or site-level "newcomer centers" can be an effective way of addressing their unique needs and accelerating their learning, bringing them to a threshold level where they can participate successfully in grade-level instruction. We caution that these programs must be carefully designed so as not to create a marginalized and segregated educational setting (Feinberg, 2000). There is a distinct risk that these programs can devolve into dumping grounds for a district's hardest-to-teach students, rather than an intensive short-term program to equip students new to the language with tools for continued content learning.

A third group of ELL students enter our school system and progress at adequate or even accelerated rates, approaching native-like proficiency as they enter secondary school. They may still sound like non-native speakers/writers of English, but they are able to interact with, comprehend, and produce grade-level work. Their language and literacy skills are in need of fine-tuning—developing knowledge about idioms, difficult grammatical structures, nuances of language, and cultural references. They can participate successfully in the mainstream academic curriculum but are still in need of focused language development.

As we look closely at the data, we see a fourth, and arguably the largest, group of English language learners who have been in the U.S. school system, perhaps since kindergarten, but have stagnated at low levels of literacy. They have reached a level of language proficiency that allows them to communicate adequately with peers in informal situations, but it does not include academic use of language. Early in their school career, we often find that these students are part of the phenomenon known as "the fourth-grade slump," where students (native English speakers and English language learners alike) who may have been maintaining pace with their peers begin to flounder as they are increasingly confronted with more rigorous academic and cognitive demands that require higher levels of comprehension and offer fewer supports for learning (Chall, Jacobs, & Baldwin, 1990). In many secondary schools, this group may comprise as much as 50 percent, or even more, of the English language learner population, greatly impacting the curriculum and instruction in the English classroom. This group of students has grown into a label all its own—Generation 1.5.

Generation 1.5

> They are in many ways marginal to both the new and old worlds, for while they straddle both worlds they are in some profound sense fully part of neither of them. (Rumbaut & Ima, 1988, p. 22)

Surprisingly, the majority of our English language learner population is native-born. According to analysis of the 2000 census data and the 2005 American Community Survey, just over 5 percent of school-age children are foreign-born, while nearly 14 percent are native-born with a foreign-born head of household (Pew Hispanic Center, 2006). These figures have significant implications when we consider that this means the large majority of these students have likely been enrolled in the U.S. school system for their entire school careers, yet they are still not proficient in English by the time they enter secondary school.

These long-term, or protracted, English language learners have come to be known as "Generation 1.5" students, a term coined in the 1980s by sociologists Rumbaut and Ima as they studied Southeast Asian refugee youth in San Diego, California. The parents of these children, who are first-generation immigrants, made a conscious decision to leave their homeland in search of a new life and brought their young children with them. As the immigrants settled in this country, many had more children, who are referred to as second generation. These children, born in the United States, tend to have a clear sense of their ethnicity and origin, stemming primarily from their parents' memories, stories, and beliefs. They typically make the shift to English fluency early on, even becoming English-dominant (Portes & Rumbaut, 2001, 2006). As they studied the Southeast Asian young people, Rumbaut and Ima recognized distinct differences between these second-generation students and their older siblings who were born in their country of origin but spent their school years in the United States. The first-generation parents are foreign-born, foreign-educated, and foreign-language dominant. Second-generation children are U.S.-born, U.S.-educated, and English dominant. Generation 1.5 students share characteristics of each group, resulting in a sometimes incongruous blend that often results in poor achievement in school.

Social versus Academic Language

Generation 1.5 children are shaped by life and school experiences from both before and after their arrival in this country. They typically left their home country during a critical period of language and academic development (Frodesen & Sasser, 2005). After six or more years in U.S. schools, they are often below grade level in reading and writing, though they may have earned passing grades in their elementary schooling, giving their families and them a false perception of their academic achievement. A more accurate picture of their achievement is revealed in their standardized test scores, which often indicate they are below basic levels of performance.

Their U.S. schooling experiences are an important factor as well. They may have received English as a Second Language (ESL or ESOL) or bilingual instruction, but generally they did not receive a consistent program and were exited early from these focused English language development experiences (Freeman & Freeman, 2002). Even those who have received ESOL instruction may not have received formal instruction in grammar or vocabulary. Instead, they have "acquired" English through informal interactions with peers, siblings, and television, rather than "learned" it in academic settings. So while they communicate adequately in everyday situations, they have not yet mastered the academic language of school. Sadly, as a result of this conversational fluency, educators and students alike may not realize that a lack of proficiency in English presents a barrier to their success in school.

Challenges in Learning

Dubarry and Alves de Lima (2003) describe three major challenges presented by this reliance on conversational language. First, as oral/aural learners, protracted English language learners tend to rely heavily on the context of oral discourse (topic, body language, facial expressions) rather than the syntactic and morphological specificity that clarifies meaning. Without understanding these cues, written discourse becomes difficult to comprehend and even more prohibitive to produce at the levels expected in secondary school.

Second, as "acquirers" of language rather than "learners" of language, they often do not notice the less salient grammatical features such as plurals, articles, prepositions, and word forms, and thus these structures do not become part of their linguistic repertoire.

Third, again as "acquirers" of language, they lack an understanding of how language works and an ability to talk about language. This "meta-language" is required in the editing and revising process of writing, and for making effective use of teacher feedback. For Generation 1.5 students, who came to the United States with limited formal schooling in their first language (due either to age or access), this lack of metalinguistic skill is particularly prominent.

It becomes the job of the English teacher, then, to bring their attention and awareness to language and literacy, providing the focused instruction and additional support in academic literacy that they require (Spaulding, 2004).

What Does It Mean to Be Proficient in a Language?

Returning to the second step in the journey toward language proficiency—knowing where you are going—we can ask, What is the end goal? What does it mean to be proficient in a language?

Approaches to language instruction have varied over the years, reflecting the primary purpose and the theoretical understandings of their time. Grammar-based instruction historically relied on explicit instruction and practice (drill) in the rules of grammar. The purpose of learning a new language was to be able to read foreign-language literature and improve native-language grammar. Accuracy was of prime importance. Methods that followed, such as the Direct Method and the Audio-Lingual Method, focused on communication and automaticity. Lessons emphasized vocabulary over the rules of grammar, which the teacher assumed the student would learn inductively after much practice using oral language (Larsen-Freeman, 2000).

Since then, we have learned much about the process of language development, recognizing the complexity of the interconnected skills needed to communicate effectively. For example, Kern (2000) offers a broad conceptual framework of language proficiency that describes three dimensions of academic literacy—linguistic, cognitive, and sociocultural. Proficient use of language requires knowledge and skill in the linguistic components. It also requires background knowledge, critical thinking and metacognitive skills, and understanding of cultural beliefs and practices. It requires skill in listening, speaking, reading, and writing to communicate in a variety of situations—academic as well as social—with a variety of audiences.

Typically, adolescent English language learners have acquired automaticity in the contextualized social language used in informal oral discourse. They have acquired this language through interaction with peers, television, and their ESL/ESOL classes, and their use of language does not vary with the situation. Of course, most ESL/ESOL classes focus on developing academic language as well as social, but often English language learners arrive in the "regular" English class still lacking the level of proficiency required to comprehend and produce grade-level work. Table 1.1 highlights the differences between the English used in everyday situations and the academic English needed in high school classes.

Proficiency Levels

As students develop language, they move through a continuum of increasing skill and understanding. TESOL (Teachers of English to Speakers of Other Languages) has developed a set of preK–12 English language proficiency standards that can guide instruction across the content areas. These five standards cross the four domains of language—listening, speaking, reading, and writing. They address the dual goals for our English language learners—proficiency in English and achievement in the core content areas (see Table 1.2).

As noted in Table 1.3, TESOL also describes five proficiency levels—entering, beginning, developing, expanding, and bridging. (Most states have developed sets of standards for these proficiency levels, though they may call them by other names, such as beginning, early intermediate, intermediate, early advanced, and advanced in California; Pre-production, Early Production, Speech Emergence, and Intermediate, or levels 1, 2, 3, 4, and 5 in other states.) The descriptors in Table 1.2 encompass four interrelated components of communication—social and academic language functions, vocabulary (word level), grammar (sentence level), and discourse (extended text level). More information about the TESOL English Language Proficiency Standards can be found at http://www.tesol.org/s_tesol/sec_document.asp?CID=1186&DID=5349.

Instructional Needs

In practical terms, these four components of language development translate into the following four specific areas of focus for classroom instruction:

Table 1.1. Differences between Everyday and Academic English

Component of Proficiency	Everyday English	Academic English
Phonological	■ Pronunciation of consonants, vowels, stress patterns	■ Irregular pronunciation and stress patterns of words borrowed from other languages ■ Spelling with regular and irregular patterns
Lexical	■ Primarily one- to two-syllable words ■ Frequently occurring words	■ Over 20,000 words ■ Words with specialized meanings that vary with context ■ Words used in a variety of forms ■ Expanded vocabulary provides specificity
Grammatical	■ Incomplete or run-on sentences are acceptable ■ Minor errors are acceptable ■ Simple structures	■ High standard of accuracy ■ Wide variety of complex structures ■ Conscious use of grammatical rules
Sociolinguistic	■ Interaction with familiar audience ■ Less complex linguistic functions: describing, questioning, etc.	■ Communication varies according to audience ■ Variety of linguistic functions: persuading, analyzing, hypothesizing, etc.
Discourse	■ Reliance on listening and speaking ■ Casual register	■ Reliance on reading and writing ■ More formal register ■ Organization varies with purpose and subject
Strategic	■ Two-way discourse provides opportunity for clarification	■ Word choice, organization of thoughts must make meaning clear
Cognitive Demands	■ Often highly contextualized ■ Centers on familiar topics	■ Fewer contextual clues ■ Centers on complex, unfamiliar topics ■ Requires more critical thinking ■ Requires extensive background knowledge

Source: Adapted from *Accelerating Academic English: A Focus on the English Learner,* by R. Scarcella, 2003 (Oakland, CA: Regents of the University of California). Used with permission.

Table 1.2. PreK–12 English Language Proficiency Standards

Standard 1	English language learners **communicate** for **social, intercultural,** and **instructional** purposes within the school setting.
Standard 2	English language learners **communicate** information, ideas, and concepts necessary for academic success in the area of **language arts.**
Standard 3	English language learners **communicate** information, ideas, and concepts necessary for academic success in the area of **mathematics.**
Standard 4	English language learners **communicate** information, ideas, and concepts necessary for academic success in the area of **science.**
Standard 5	English language learners **communicate** information, ideas, and concepts necessary for academic success in the area of **social studies.**

Source: *PreK–12 English Language Proficiency Standards* by TESOL. Copyright 2006 by Teachers of English to Speakers of Other Languages. Reproduced with permission of Teachers of English to Speakers of Other Languages in the format Textbook via Copyright Clearance Center.

- **Vocabulary**: the technical language needed to read, write, and talk about the content areas in literature, math, science, social studies.
- **Grammar**: the linguistic complexity needed to comprehend grade-level written and oral discourse, and to produce coherent, cohesive written assignments.
- **Fluency**: the ability to recognize and produce the sounds of English and to use precise language to express ideas. Fluency in reading is necessary to follow and comprehend text. Fluency in writing is needed to convey understanding and original thought in a more formal context.
- **Comprehension**: the ability to understand high levels of vocabulary and complex linguistic and text structures that present familiar and unfamiliar concepts.

The four focus chapters in this book describe the unique challenges for English language learners in these areas and provide practical, research-based strategies for instruction. Each chapter defines and illustrates an approach that integrates the four domains of language—reading, writing, listening, and speaking—with the teaching and learning of grade-level English language arts content and standards.

Conclusion

Developing proficiency in language, literacy, and content is a multifaceted process that requires knowledge of our students, knowledge of language and language development, and knowledge of the pedagogy

Table 1.3. Performance Definitions of the Five Levels of English Language Proficiency (TESOL)

Level 1 Starting	Level 2 Emerging	Level 3 Developing	Level 4 Expanding	Level 5 Bridging
English language learners can understand and use the following:				
Language to communicate with others around basic concrete needs	Language to draw on simple and routine experiences to communicate with others	Language to communicate with others on familiar matters regularly encountered	Language in both concrete and abstract situations and apply language to new experiences	A wide range of longer oral and written texts and recognize implicit meaning
High-frequency words and memorized chunks of language	High-frequency and some general academic vocabulary and expressions	General and some specialized academic vocabulary and expressions	Specialized and some technical academic vocabulary and expressions	Technical academic vocabulary and expressions
Words, phrases, or chunks of language	Phrases or short sentences in oral or written communication	Expanded sentences in oral or written communication	A variety of sentence lengths of varying linguistic complexity in oral and written communication	A variety of sentence lengths of varying linguistic complexity in extended oral or written discourse
Pictorial, graphic, or nonverbal representation language	Oral or written language, making errors that often impede the meaning of the communication	Oral or written language, making errors that may impede the communication but retain much of its meaning	Oral or written language, making minimal errors that do not impede the overall meaning of the communication	Oral or written language approaching comparability to that of English-proficient peers

Source: *PreK–12 English Language Proficiency Standards* by TESOL. Copyright 2006 by Teachers of English to Speakers of Other Languages. Reproduced with permission of Teachers of English to Speakers of Other Languages in the format Textbook via Copyright Clearance Center.

of developing literacy from the early stages through the advanced. As we travel on this journey with our students, it is helpful to keep in mind the two types of relationships in which we are involved—the teacher and learner and the adult and adolescent. The teacher-learner relationship revolves around language, literacy, and content (NCTE, 2006). The adult-adolescent relationship revolves around personal and family issues. This requires knowing our students as learners and as members of a larger community outside of school. When we focus on both types of relationships, we can help to bridge the gap between school and the often very different world in which our English language learners live. As Arian described in her essay, learning English is not as much a linear path as it is an increasing expansion of their worlds. For adolescent language learners, life's circular path is as large or as small as their language will take them. As English teachers, it is our role to make that circle as encompassing as possible.

2 Teaching and Learning in English: What Works

I was scare. I thought nobody spoken Spanish. I just could hear this weird sound. I would see the sign—it was like I wasn't literate. It was like starting all over again, starting with the basics. I will start learning how to count, it will be like being in elementary school even though I was in high school.

Raquel Ramirez, college sophomore

Raquel is one of our success stories. Arriving in the United States at the age of fourteen, she completed high school in four years and is now beginning her sophomore year at the university with a double major in psychology and criminal justice. Her college grade point average is 3.68, and based on her test scores she was not required to take any college remedial courses. As she tells the story of her first day in high school, her words paint a clear picture of exactly what she wanted to express—the anxiety, fear, and frustration of coming to a new country and attending school using a new language. These words also highlight the variance of her ability to use English. On the one hand she easily uses high-level vocabulary, complex sentence structures, and idiomatic expressions. Still, she struggles with basic verb tenses and pronunciation. This unevenness in proficiency points to a need for standards that set high expectations supported through a model of instruction that addresses individual needs.

Beginning with the Standards

Given the diversity of our students, it can be tempting to be satisfied with even small amounts of improvement in skills and understanding. We are reluctant to point out all the errors a student makes in his or her writing. We're happy when our students get the "big idea" from a piece of text, but we may not expect them to evaluate credibility and comprehensiveness of evidence or analyze the way in which the author establishes the tone of the text. We may be satisfied when students write a paper with a coherent thesis that maintains focus, without expecting them to improve that coherence through a clear organization of thoughts or precise word choice.

The English language arts (ELA) content standards are just as important for our English language learners as they are for our native speakers. Using them in their entirety ensures that we hold the same high expectations for all our students, regardless of their language proficiency level. However, it does not mean that teaching should proceed without regard to language proficiency. The English Language Development (ELD) or English Language Proficiency (ELP) standards provide a road map to the ELA standards, describing performance indicators of progress at each level of proficiency. State ELD standards or TESOL's ELP standards (see Chapter 1) can be used in conjunction with the ELA standards to guide planning, instruction, and assessment.

What Makes Learning in English Difficult for Adolescent English Language Learners?

Successful participation in any academic activity, whether oral or written, is a complex process that involves more than the match between the proficiency level of the learner and the difficulty level of the text. In other words, simply providing secondary school students with leveled books (e.g., beginners using texts written at a primary grade level) will not result in significant improvements in language learning. Rather, teachers must be sure to consider all of the influences on comprehension. Aida Walqui (2002, p. 2) identifies key elements that we interpret as three primary factors that impact a student's ability to engage in the lesson:

- **The Learner**: language proficiency, knowledge of vocabulary, background experiences, prior knowledge about the topic, motivation and interest.
- **The Text**: complexity of ideas, features and structures, sentence complexity, density of ideas, text coherence (elaboration, explanation, expression of relationships between ideas, visual and textual supports). Note: the word *text* used here refers to both written and oral narrative and exposition.
- **The Context**: purpose for reading, writing or speaking, instructional activities and scaffolds.

The three elements described above pertain to all learners. Within this construct, however, we find that an English language learner often possesses an idiosyncratic knowledge and experience profile that can present unique challenges, especially when it comes to familiarity with the linguistic code, text structures, and rhetorical styles. We explore each of these challenges below.

Lack of Familiarity with the Linguistic Code

Clearly, language is one of the greatest factors in being able to comprehend text and participate in academic tasks. The linguistic code comprises the phonology, the lexicon, the grammar, sociolinguistics, and discourse patterns and practices (Scarcella, 2003). While each of these aspects of the linguistic code may present difficulties for even native speakers of English, certain aspects are of particular concern in teaching English language learners.

Pronunciation. A lack of familiarity with the sounds of English can lead to difficulty in making oneself understood in conversation due to pronunciation. Inaccurate pronunciation can also lead to inaccurate spelling. When students don't hear the *-ed* ending of a word or are unable to differentiate between vowel sounds, it shows up in their writing. Raquel wrote "I was scare," and we can clearly see by the verb tense that she intended to say "I was scared." Errors such as this go beyond the expected difficulty that native speakers experience in learning tenses. Even among advanced English language learners such as Raquel, they may not perceive all the phonemes in words, thus forcing them to rely on their ability to recall rules when using these words in their writing. This can be further complicated by the many exceptions to English spelling patterns that stem from an abundance of words borrowed from many different languages.

Vocabulary. In primary school, students learn the "five-finger rule" for selecting independent reading materials: if they count more than five unfamiliar words on a single page, the book is too difficult, and they should select another. This is a good reminder to us about the link between understanding vocabulary and the content itself. Dutro and Moran (2003) discuss vocabulary in two distinct categories: mortar and bricks. The "mortar" of a piece of text—signal words, transition devices, negative markers, pronouns, and articles—are as important as the "bricks"—the technical vocabulary or the key words. They interact to express important relationships between ideas. After all, loving someone is different from being in love with someone. As English teachers, the temptation is to teach the word *love*, since that is the focus of those phrases. Yet a lack of understanding of the interaction of the brick word (*love*) with the mortar words (*in, with*) surrounding it leads to a loss of meaning. Therefore, a lack of familiarity with some of the most basic English vocabulary can seriously impede comprehension.

Even students with more advanced proficiency may get the gist of a conversation or of a reading but may miss the nuances because of the amount of unfamiliar vocabulary. Nuances in vocabulary may be the key to recognizing the author's purpose or bias, both of which are essential skills found in secondary school English language arts standards.

Idioms present another area of difficulty for English language learners. We use them unconsciously in our speech, sometimes as a way of explaining an idea we want students to understand, such as "a loose cannon" to describe a character's unpredictable and embarrassing behavior. Native English speakers grow up hearing and using idioms and can interpret them as they come across them in texts, but a student who is unfamiliar with an idiomatic expression will not be able to understand it simply by deconstructing it. Words and expressions are a reflection of culture and values that may be different from a student's own. The word *time*, for instance, is the most often used noun in the English language (Soanes & Stevenson, 2006). It is a critical concept in organizing a variety of literary and expository genres. We expect students to be able to organize events and ideas chronologically in a linear view of time. Not all cultures tell a story in this linear pattern; not all languages express the passage of time in the same manner. Vietnamese, for instance, uses auxiliaries rather than tense to signal past or future events, as in "work yesterday" (Bliss, 2001).

Grammar. Students must also have a good grasp of the grammatical structures found in academic text, structures not frequently used in everyday English. Clear writing and speaking depends on adept use of passive and active voice, conditional tense, dependent clauses, and gerundial phrases, among others. Without grammar, vocabulary becomes a string of unrelated words. Calling attention to and explicitly teaching these structures as they are found in the text will help English language learners make sense out of the string of words.

Register. Acceptable ways of communicating with different audiences are bound by culture and marked by word choice, tone, and even grammatical structures. Students from diverse linguistic and cultural backgrounds may not be familiar with the subtleties of language patterns that change depending on the audience, purpose, or topic. Reading an essay from a standard English learner can be like listening to a casual conversation between friends, full of tangential details, word choice that is not appropriate for school, and a personal tone that may be out of place in an academic piece. Both standard English learners and English language learners benefit from direct instruction in the registers used in writing, classroom discussions, and oral presentations.

Lack of Familiarity with Text Structures and Features

There are five common text patterns that we use to express logical connections: description, sequence, compare/contrast, cause and effect, and problem/solution. Each of these patterns has specific signal words that help the reader recognize the particular type of organization and thus the relationships between the important ideas. Text features such as headings, charts, and diagrams in the text support the connections between ideas. Students who are not familiar with the structures and features of text will have more difficulty linking ideas and constructing meaning as new information is presented. Students can use graphic organizers to make the structure of the text transparent and comprehensible. They can also use them as a scaffold to create their own compositions, jotting down the key events or concepts in the appropriate section of the graphic organizer, adding in applicable signal words, and then composing well-organized, cohesive text supported with evidence and details. Table 2.1 provides an overview of the types of text features commonly found in informational readings.

Table 2.1. Common Text Features

Organization of Text	■ Table of contents ■ Index ■ Glossary ■ Page numbers
Organization of Ideas	■ Synopses (beginning or end of reading) ■ Titles ■ Headings ■ Subheadings ■ Conclusion
Graphic Aids	■ Photographs ■ Illustrations ■ Diagrams ■ Charts and tables ■ Maps
Elaboration Emphasis	■ Captions ■ Bold, italicized, or highlighted words ■ Footnotes ■ Margin notes
Extension of Understanding	■ Questions

Diverse Rhetorical Styles

> You don't want to depress your audience by giving everything away immediately. And you don't want to bore them either, so you do what is considered interesting, which is to give plenty of details and a conversational tone to your written text. (Brazilian English language learner quoted in Fox, 1994, p. 22)

The discourse component of the linguistic code is inextricably entwined with culture. English language learners come from diverse cultural backgrounds with diverse perspectives on logic and organization of thought. In English we expect a linear development of thought. Inductive reasoning provides details that lead to a conclusion, while texts utilizing deductive reasoning begin with a thesis and then provide details to support it. Other cultures develop ideas quite differently. Determining relevance or irrelevance of details, deciding how to organize an essay or formulate an argument is not universal but rather is culturally defined (Leki, 1992). This has significant implications for constructing paragraphs, determining importance, and establishing coherence. Imagine what an essay written by the Brazilian student quoted above might look like. This conversational tone might be an appropriate way to deliver a message in Brazil, but it would be unacceptable in an expository essay comparing and contrasting McCarthyism with Arthur Miller's play *The Crucible.*

A primary focus in the English class is teaching students how to construct first a paragraph and then an essay. English language arts standards address a variety of narrative and expository genres in writing. And most students, native speakers included, need a great deal of direct instruction and practice in writing (Frey & Fisher, 2006). For English language learners, there is an added dimension in that the rhetorical styles in their culture may differ widely from those expected in their classrooms. These differences have implications for reading, writing, listening, and speaking. Academic writing in English is generally organized around an overt statement of a thesis, supported by reasons, examples, and details. See Table 2.2 to see how a persuasive argument can be presented differently in different cultures. Although these are generalizations about the organization of ideas in other cultures, a native English-speaking reader (teacher) might find a student's essay inadequate and make comments such as "missed the point," "talked around the point," "failed to connect the thesis and the evidence," or "failed to present validity of the argument," when, in fact, the student is presenting the argument in a culturally different rhetorical style.

Anna Söter (1988) analyzed narrative writing by eleventh-grade native speakers of Arabic, Vietnamese, and English in Australia. They were asked to write a bedtime story for a young child. All the stories contained the major elements that we consider important—setting, action, character. The differences lay in the emphasis on each of these. The stories of the native English speakers portrayed a strong sense of action and plot. The stories from the Vietnamese speakers included a greater proportion of dialogue, describing the relationships between characters and feelings. And the setting received more attention in the stories of the Arabic students.

Other studies have shown differences in the perception of the purpose of a narrative. Indrasuta (1988) found that American students felt the purpose of a narrative was to entertain and inform, and therefore their goal was to capture the interest of the reader. In contrast, Thai students saw the purpose as teaching morals and thought their stories had to be true stories. We can easily see that these cultural beliefs might create writing that does not meet the teacher's expectations. It also can mean that students focus on different aspects of text as they read, per-

Table 2.2. Diverse Rhetorical Styles and Expectations of Academic English in Persuasive Essays

Language	Elements of Rhetorical Style
African American Vernacular	■ Rely on rhythm and repetition to persuade
Japanese	■ Consider it rude to tell reader what to do or believe ■ Make points in favor of, or against, without direct statement of intent
Korean	■ Provide points related to the argument, repeat using some previously stated points and introduce new ideas ■ Repeat several times, each time adding or eliminating ideas, expecting reader to infer the main point
Lakota	■ Tell related stories ■ May not mention the thesis
Spanish	■ Use passive voice and passive reflective verbs ("The book lost itself to me") ■ Cautious description

Source: Adapted from "Rhetorical Structures for Multilingual and Multicultural Students" by A. Bliss, 2001. *Contrastive Rhetoric Revisited and Redefined* (Paper) by Bliss, A. Copyright 2000 by Lawrence Erlbaum Associates Inc. – Books. Reproduced with permission of Lawrence Erlbaum Associates Inc. – Books in the format Textbook via Copyright Clearance Center.

haps missing key elements the teacher wants them to notice and understand.

Courtney Cazden (1988) described a project in which white adults and African American adults were asked to listen to recordings of stories written by white first graders and by African American first graders. Based solely on these stories, they were asked to predict the children's future success in school. The white adults found one of the stories of the African American children to be incoherent and predicted that the child "might have trouble reading," commenting on language problems that would affect achievement. The African American adults noticed the nonlinear quality of the story but found it "well-formed, easy to understand" (p. 18). They pronounced the child to be bright and verbal and predicted that she would be successful in school.

Lack of Requisite Background Knowledge

English language learners also come to school with a wide variety of background experiences and levels of knowledge about any given topic. One high school English teacher asked her students to read a short story that made reference to Grand Central Station. Although many students may not be familiar with this particular train station, two of her students who had recently arrived from the Marshall Islands did not know what a train station was. In too many classrooms, background knowledge is assumed and therefore not activated and developed. As Marzano (2004) noted, building background knowledge is one of the most important things teachers can do to improve reading. In fact, there is evidence that students who have significant background knowledge on a specific topic can even comprehend texts that are poorly written or very complex.

Background knowledge is bound by culture, by experience, and by prior learning. Students who have not attended elementary school in the United States will likely have had far less exposure to events we often assume our students know about, such as the westward movement or industrialization. They may have gaps in their knowledge about pivotal time periods that have had a profound influence on literature, such as the Renaissance. Students who come from war-torn countries where dictatorships limit personal freedom may be unfamiliar with concepts of democracy and freedom of speech. These values are imbued in our classroom practices as well as our content, and students may need direct instruction to build background knowledge before engaging in the unit of study.

Effective Practice: Review of Research

Numerous agencies and organizations have examined current practice in developing language and literacy in English language learners. They have visited schools, convened panels of experts, analyzed existing research, and compiled lengthy reports of their findings. While each report brings a different perspective, the consistency of their findings is at once striking and telling. In sum, they paint a picture of effective practice that is standards-based and assessment-driven, immerses students in language, recognizes the diversity of proficiency and background, considers the primary language, teaches metacognitive strategies side by side with reading and writing skills, and integrates reading, writing, listening, and speaking with content learning. We present the highlights from several of these important documents below.

Best Practices in Academic Literacy for Immigrant Secondary School Students

Spaulding, Carolino, and Amen (2004) identified specific practices that teachers should implement to address the needs of English language learners, including:

1. Recognize the different linguistic and academic needs of students in various ELL subpopulations.
2. Use the native language to support English language development.
3. Implement language development standards and assessments that are directly linked to academic standards and assessments.
4. Create literacy-rich secondary school environments.
5. Use instructional approaches that unify language and content learning.
6. Instruct students in language learning strategies. (p. 25)

Developing Literacy in English Language Learners

The National Literacy Panel on Language-Minority Children and Youth (August & Shanahan, 2006) conducted an in-depth review of the research on developing literacy in English language learners. Their findings identify successful practices at the same time as they reveal some significant gaps in our knowledge about this topic. We have summarized their findings below.

1. *Instruction in the key components of reading—phonemic awareness, phonics, fluency, vocabulary, and text comprehension.* English language learners improve their literacy when these key compo-

nents are taught simultaneously. Consideration for language proficiency level and features of the primary language (e.g., the sounds that differ between home and school language or false cognates between the two languages) helps teachers modify approaches used with native English speakers.

2. *Instruction in these key components is not sufficient to develop proficiency in reading and writing. Oral proficiency in English is critical as well.* English language learners generally attain parity with native English speakers in word-level skills such as decoding, word recognition, spelling. Their text-level skills (reading comprehension and writing) lag significantly behind their native-speaking peers. The research suggests that this disparity stems from a lack of proficiency in oral language. Oral proficiency of vocabulary knowledge, listening comprehension, syntactic skills, and metalinguistic skills is strongly correlated to proficiency in reading and writing.
3. *Oral proficiency and literacy in the first language can be used to facilitate literacy development in English.* Students who are literate in their first language will generally develop English proficiency more rapidly and more easily than those who are not. They can transfer their knowledge and skills from their primary language as they develop language and literacy in an additional language. Older students are able to rely on metalinguistic skills to assist them in learning another language (Zadina, 2005). For example, recognizing cognates (words that have similar spellings and meanings in two languages) can help students develop vocabulary easily.
4. *Individual differences contribute significantly to English literacy development.* Developing literacy is a dynamic process influenced by many factors including proficiency in the first language and in English, the student's age, cognitive abilities, prior knowledge, and experiences, and the similarities and differences between the primary language and English.
5. *Home language experiences can have a positive impact on literacy achievement.* Not surprisingly, students perform better when they are learning in their stronger language. Finding ways to bridge the gap between home and school patterns of interaction can increase engagement and motivation. Text that is culturally meaningful can facilitate comprehension.

In addition to the conclusions this panel was able to make, they also identified two areas in which the profession still needs information:

1. *An understanding of how sociocultural contexts impact literacy development.* Existing studies do little to define the impact on literacy development of sociocultural variables such as immigration status, discourse patterns, family influences, district, state, and federal policies, and language status. Some research

suggests correlations but do not define them through empirical evidence.

2. *Ways to assess student progress for instructional planning.* Formal and informal assessments are fundamental to making placement decisions and planning instruction. For the most part, current methods of assessment are inadequate for these purposes, and studies that examine these methods are flawed in their approach. It does appear that when teachers are asked to respond to specific criteria as opposed to expressing a spontaneous opinion, they provide information that is helpful in planning.

NCTE Position Paper on the Role of English Teachers in Educating English Language Learners

The National Council of Teachers of English (NCTE, 2006) has detailed effective practices for teaching English language learners. They focus on three areas within the English classroom: teaching language, teaching reading, and teaching writing. We present each of these areas in Figures 2.1, 2.2, and 2.3, respectively. Taken together, these components of the NCTE position statement clearly illustrate the needs of English language learners and ways in which students can best learn. Importantly, NCTE also recognizes that language and content reinforce one another. Simply focusing on language development with adolescent English language learners will not result in the achievement gains we expect. "The best way to help students learn both English and the knowledge of school subjects is to teach language through content. This should

- Recognize that second language acquisition is a gradual developmental process and is built on students knowledge and skill in their native language.
- Provide authentic opportunities to use language in a nonthreatening environment.
- Teach key vocabulary connected with the topic of the lesson.
- Teach academic oral language in the context of various content areas.
- Teach text- and sentence-level grammar in context to help students understand the structure and style of the English language.
- Teach the specific features of language students need to communicate in social as well as academic contexts.

Figure 2.1. Teaching language. *Source*: Adapted from *Position Paper on the Role of English Teachers in Educating English Language Learners (ELLs),* by National Council of Teachers of English, 2006 (Urbana, IL: Author).

- Provide reading materials that are culturally relevant.
- Connect the readings with the students background knowledge and experiences.
- Encourage students to discuss the readings, including the cultural dimensions of the text.
- Have students read a more accessible text on the topic before reading the assigned text.
- Ask families to read with students a version in the heritage language.
- Replace discrete skill exercises and drills with many opportunities to read.
- Provide opportunities for silent reading in either the students first language or in English.
- Read aloud frequently to allow students to become familiar with and appreciate the sounds and structures of written language.
- Read aloud while students have access to the text to facilitate connecting oral and written modalities.
- Activate students background knowledge of the text before introducing the text.
- Teach language features such as text structure, vocabulary, and text- and sentence-level grammar to facilitate comprehension of the text.
- Recognize that first and second language growth increases with abundant reading and writing.
- Relate the topic to the cultural experiences of the students.
- "Front load" comprehension via a walk through the text or a preview of the main ideas, and other strategies that prepare students for the topic of the text.
- Do prereading activities that elicit discussion of the topic.
- Teach key vocabulary essential for the topic.
- Recognize that experiences in writing can be used to clarify understanding of reading.

Figure 2.2. Teaching literacy: reading. *Source*: Adapted from *Position Paper on the Role of English Teachers in Educating English Language Learners (ELLs),* by National Council of Teachers of English, 2006 (Urbana, IL: Author).

not replace reading and writing instruction in English, nor study of literature and grammar" (NCTE, 2006, pp. 6–7).

Using content to teach language provides a natural context for developing language and literacy, even as it builds vocabulary and background knowledge for learning in the content area. This is especially important given the limited amount of time students have to attain grade-level standards across the curriculum. It provides an authentic

- Provide a nurturing environment for writing.
- Assign cooperative, collaborative writing activities that promote discussion.
- Encourage contributions from all students and promote peer interaction to support learning.
- Replace drills and single-response exercises with time for writing practice.
- Provide frequent meaningful opportunities for students to generate their own texts.
- Design writing assignments for a variety of audiences, purposes, and genres, and scaffold the writing instruction.
- Provide models of well-organized papers for the class. Use sample papers to model specific aspects of the paper that make it well written.
- Comment on strengths in order to indicate areas where the student is meeting expectations.
- Make comments explicit and clear (both in written response and in oral responses). Begin feedback with global comments (content and ideas, organization, thesis) and then move on to more local concerns (or mechanical errors) when student writers are more confident with the content of their draft.
- Give more than one suggestion for change—so that students still maintain control of their writing.
- Teach students how to cite references. Teach the values that are implicit in the rules of plagiarism and textual borrowing, noting that not all cultures ascribe to the same rules and guidelines.°Teach strategies for avoiding plagiarism.

Figure 2.3. Teaching literacy: writing. *Source*: Adapted from *Position Paper on the Role of English Teachers in Educating English Language Learners (ELLs)*, by National Council of Teachers of English, 2006 (Urbana, IL: Author).

purpose for language practice and offers the redundancy of language and concepts that allows students to develop understanding through multiple interactions with the same language and ideas (Walqui, 2002).

Reading Next: Key Elements of Effective Reading Instruction

A panel of experts invited by the Carnegie Foundation identified fifteen critical components for improving adolescent literary. Each was derived from a strong research base of instructional and infrastructural practices found to be effective in middle and high schools (Biancarosa & Snow, 2004). Teaching reading to adolescent struggling readers is a different proposition from teaching reading in elementary school. For most, it is not an issue of being able to read words accurately, but rather one of comprehension. And with the wide diversity of students' background and skill, that inability to comprehend what they read stems from a wide variety of reasons. Some may lack the fluency required to comprehend, while others may not know comprehension strategies such as predicting, summarizing, or inferring. We often find that English language learners have not had enough practice with enough different kinds of text to be able to use these strategies independently and apply them in different subject areas. They may not have an adequate vocabulary or relevant background knowledge to make meaning from the text.

In Tables 2.3 and 2.4 we have listed these findings along with specific implications for teaching English language learners.

Writing Next: Key Elements of Effective Writing Instruction

In their synthesis of research on writing, Graham and Perin (2007) identified eleven elements effective for helping adolescents learn to write well and to use writing as a tool for learning. Writing well is difficult for many students, not just English language learners. It is perhaps the most difficult of the four domains of language because it requires students to integrate skills from oral language and reading in order to compose a well-organized, fluent expression of their ideas. Constructing a complete and cohesive essay requires that students have extensive background knowledge and a deep understanding of their topic. They must understand the unique characteristics of each genre and what is required to achieve the desired goal. They must be able to use a high-level academic lexicon as well as more common vocabulary such as transition words, pronouns, and prepositions.

In Table 2.5 we have listed the eleven elements, a brief explanation of each, and particular considerations for English language learners.

Double the Work: Challenges and Solutions for Acquiring Language and Academic Literacy

In the newest report on the subject of English language learners, at least at the time of this writing, Short and Fitzsimmons (2007, p. 14) identified six major challenges in improving adolescent ELL literacy:

1. Lack of common criteria for identifying and tracking their academic performance.
2. Lack of appropriate assessments.
3. Inadequate educator capacity for improving literacy of language learners.
4. Lack of appropriate and flexible program options.
5. Inadequate use of research-based instructional practices.
6. Lack of a strong and coherent research agenda about adolescent English language learners' literacy instruction.

Table 2.3. Key Elements of Effective Reading Instruction, Focusing on English Language Learners

Instructional Practice	Explanation	Focus on ELL
Direct, explicit comprehension instruction	Teach the strategies and processes that proficient readers use to understand what they read	▪ Model, model, model! ▪ Elaborate instruction rather than simplify
Effective instructional principles embedded in content	Use content-area texts in language arts classes and teach content-area-specific reading and writing skills in content classes	▪ Use content as a vehicle to teach language—students do not learn language in a vacuum ▪ Incorporate language teaching throughout the day, throughout the content areas to accelerate learning
Motivation and self-directed learning	Build motivation to read and learn and provide students with the instruction and supports needed for independent learning tasks they will face after graduation	▪ Teach students to take responsibility for learning and re-engage as active, not passive, learners ▪ Provide choice in text selection ▪ Provide varied levels of texts on a common topic
Text-based collaborative learning	Encourage students to interact with one another around a variety of texts	▪ Group students heterogeneously to provide language models and scaffolds for learning when students are working with one another on collaborative tasks
Strategic tutoring	Provide students with intense individualized reading, writing, and content instruction as needed	▪ Group students homogeneously to address like needs and develop language proficiency when the teacher or tutor is present
Diverse texts	Use texts at a variety of difficulty levels and on a variety of topics	▪ Ensure access for ELLs through differentiated texts that address the same topic ▪ Incorporate texts from a variety of cultural perspectives
Intensive writing instruction	Connect to the kinds of writing tasks students will have to perform in high school and beyond	▪ Assign tasks that require high-level critical thinking skills and teach the language and strategies needed to analyze, synthesize, justify, persuade, etc. ▪ Scaffold writing instruction through talk, visuals, graphic organizers, writing frames, and gradual release of responsibility
Technology	Use as a tool for and a topic of literacy instruction	▪ Use technology to scaffold understanding through visuals and access to a variety of sources
Ongoing formative assessment	Learn how they are progressing under current instructional practices	▪ Assess all four domains of language—reading, writing, speaking, and listening ▪ Provide focused, selective feedback that differentiates between language and content

Table 2.4. Key Elements of an Infrastructure That Supports Effective Reading Instruction

Instructional Practice	Explanation	Focus on ELL
Extended time for literacy	Two to four hours of instruction and practice in language arts and content-area classes	■ Provide additional instructional time for ELLs to close the gap—learn language and content
Professional development	Both long term and ongoing	■ Include focus on language and the language acquisition process
Ongoing summative assessment	Assess students and programs, to provide data that are reported for accountability and research purposes	■ Assess in relation to both ELA and ELD/ELP standards
Interdisciplinary teacher teams	Meet regularly to discuss students and align instruction	■ Organize instruction thematically to provide redundancy of language, vocabulary, and ideas
Leadership	Provide guidance from principals and teachers who have a solid understanding of how to teach reading and writing to the full array of students	■ Use data to plan purposeful placement and instruction of ELL ■ Understand how ELL needs differ from native speakers
A comprehensive and coordinated literacy program	Coordinate between disciplines and departments, out-of-school organizations, and the local community	■ Teach reading across the content to contextualize skills and concepts, provide redundancy of language and ideas, connect to prior learning and experience

As you can imagine, these are formidable challenges. Thankfully, the authors of this report also proposed a number of potential solutions. Their solutions have been incorporated into the very fabric of this book. In fact, we were motivated to write this book following the site visit Shannon Fitzsimmons conducted at Hoover High School. The solutions found in *Double the Work* have been the focus of our work there. These recommendations suggest that we as English educators should do the following:

- *Integrate all four language skills from the start.* In far too many classrooms, English language learners are not provided instruction in reading and writing until they have developed basic oral proficiency. In other classrooms, oral language is not developed and used in conjunction with reading and writing.
- *Teach the components and processes of reading and writing.* Some English language learners may need to learn the sounds of English or the vocabulary terms for a specific topic. As teachers,

Table 2.5. Key Elements of Effective Writing Instruction, Focusing on English Language Learners

Instructional Practice	Explanation	Focus on ELL
Writing strategies	Teach students strategies to plan, revise, and edit their compositions	■ Teach the organization of various genres—organization of writing can vary from culture to culture ■ Teach the vocabulary and language structures that make the thesis and evidence clear
Summarization	Explicitly and systematically teach students to summarize texts	■ Use graphic organizers to help ELLs chunk text for summarizing
Collaborative writing	Use instructional arrangements in which students work together to plan, draft, revise, and edit their compositions	■ Provide opportunities for students to practice oral language—listening and speaking—to hear and rehearse models of language they can transfer to writing
Specific product goals	Assign students specific, reachable goals for the writing they will complete	■ Break down goals as needed to make writing less overwhelming for students who are learning language at the same time as writing strategies
Word processing	Use computers as instructional supports for writing assignments	■ Teach students to use spell-check and online thesaurus dictionaries (including primary language) ■ Provide prescreened websites for research
Sentence combining	Teach students to construct increasingly complex, sophisticated sentences	■ Use this as a way to teach grammar in context
Prewriting	Engage students in activities designed to help them generate and organize their ideas for compositions	■ Provide opportunities that encourage students to practice oral language
Inquiry activities	Engage students in analyzing data to help them develop ideas and content for a particular writing task	■ Assure that ELLs are engaged in tasks that require high-level critical thinking
Process writing approach	Integrate a number of writing instructional activities in a workshop that focuses on extended writing opportunities, writing for authentic audiences and purposes, personalized instruction, and cycles of writing	■ Provide daily opportunities to practice writing ■ Link assignments to personal experience to activate background knowledge
Study of models	Provide students with opportunities to read, analyze, and emulate models of good writing	■ Provide numerous models before expecting students to produce independently
Writing for content learning	Use writing as a tool for learning content material	■ Provide opportunities to talk with peers before asking students to write ■ Build background knowledge before asking students to write

we must provide instruction in these components. However, focusing solely on the components will not result in proficient and skilled readers and writers. Adolescent English language learners also need to engage in the processes of reading and writing, as well as learning the language required to summarize, synthesize, discuss, draft, respond, revise, and evaluate.

- *Teach reading comprehension strategies.* Adolescents need instruction, modeling, and coaching in the use of comprehension strategies. Their age alone is not an indicator that they have mastered the skills necessary to understand and think critically about texts. When the language or the content of a text is unfamiliar, it becomes even more important to use these strategies to facilitate understanding.
- *Focus on vocabulary development.* Many students will develop a conversational vocabulary as they engage with peers, TV, and society. However, without instruction they cannot develop an academic vocabulary. English language learners need multiple exposures and opportunities to use new vocabulary. Context clues alone are often insufficient to assist ELLs in making meaning because they do not understand enough of the surrounding text.
- *Build and activate background knowledge.* A number of researchers, policy analysts, and teachers have come to the same conclusion: background knowledge is a significant predictor of reading comprehension and future learning. As such, a focus on background knowledge is essential in every lesson we teach.
- *Teach language through content and themes.* Focusing on language in the absence of content not only is more difficult but is also less motivating for students. Adolescents want to know why they're learning what they're asked to learn; they ask about relevance all of the time. They also enjoy discussing big ideas and engaging in inquiry, which naturally requires language. Combining language and content ensures that students develop their linguistic competence and content knowledge while being connected to the world around them. Organizing instruction around important themes provides the redundancy that is critical to learning language. As ideas are presented from a variety of perspectives, students have multiple opportunities to hear and use the same language.

There is an amazing amount of consistency across these reports. First, they all clearly demonstrate that teachers matter and that what they do can either facilitate or hinder the progress of English language learners. Second, they point to specific instructional interventions, procedures, strategies, and systems that teachers can use to ensure students' success. Third, they each suggest that literacy is complex and that literacy development requires purposeful instruction. They also note that focusing on isolated skills will not work. And finally, they point to the knowledge that effective teachers have and need to have if they are to be successful.

Before we turn our attention to the language focus areas that adolescent English language learners need—grammar, vocabulary, fluency, and comprehension—let's focus on the instructional routines and procedures necessary to accelerate language and literacy learning.

A Model for Organizing Instruction for English Language Learners

> "That's the reason they're called lessons," the Gryphon remarked: "because they lessen from day to day." (Lewis Carroll, *Alice's Adventures in Wonderland,* 1865)

Carroll raises an interesting point: our instruction should decrease over time. This idea was further developed by Pearson and Gallagher (1983) through the gradual release of responsibility model of instruction. The model suggests that the teacher moves from assuming "all the responsibility for performing a task . . . to a situation in which the students assume all of the responsibility" (Duke & Pearson, 2002, p. 211). Stated another way, "The Gradual Release model emphasizes instruction that mentors students into becoming capable thinkers and learners when handling the tasks with which they have not yet developed expertise" (Buehl, 2005, para. 15).

In her book *Other People's Children,* Delpit (1996) describes the support learners get from other people and from books:

> Think about the difference between learning to play chess from your grandfather or learning from a book. The best part about learning from a grandfather is that there is presumably a relationship to build the learning on and, because he is there with you, he can adjust the instruction according to what he sees that you need. The problem with depending on a grandfather is that you might not have one when you need one. (p. 96)

Without using the term, Delpit describes one of the essential features of the gradual release of responsibility model—that the teacher can adjust instruction. This is a critical feature and one that we cannot forget if we are going to see appreciable changes in the literacy performance of our English language learners.

A visual of our implementation of the gradual release of responsibility model can be found in Figure 2.4. We have identified four broad categories of instruction (Frey & Fisher, 2006). Over time, and with purposeful instruction and support in each of these categories, information, strategies, skills, content, and language transfer from the teacher or knowledgeable other to the student.

Focus Lessons. In this phase of instruction, the teacher models thinking or information for the whole class. The teacher does not ask students to provide answers, but the teacher may have a conversation with the class. This is the "I do it" phase in which the teacher does almost all of the work. In general, the focus lessons should clearly establish the purpose for the day, week, or theme. We know that English language learners learn more and faster when they understand the purpose of the lesson (Hill & Flynn, 2006). The focus lesson is often a shared reading and think-aloud in which the teacher models his or her thinking about a piece of text. In doing so, the teacher does the following:

- builds students' vocabulary
- models vocabulary learning through context clues or word parts
- develops students' understanding of fluent reading
- models fluent reading, punctuation, and intonation
- uses standard grammar
- focuses the students' attention on examples of targeted language structures

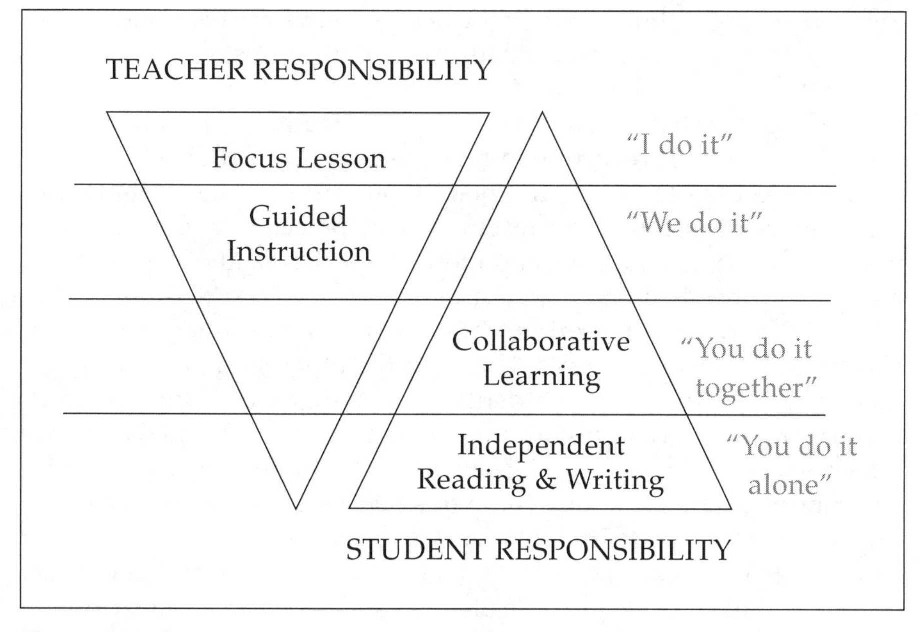

Figure 2.4. Gradual release of responsibility model.

- shares examples of comprehension strategy use
- models comprehension skills

While the focus lesson is a critical component of instruction, it cannot last too long. In general, adolescents will continue to learn in this format for about fifteen minutes. Any longer than that and students will likely lose interest, become confused, forget the point or purpose, and disengage.

Guided Instruction. Over many years of work in literacy, we have come to believe that students will never learn to read or write well if they spend period after period in whole class groups. We know that the "real teaching" that we do in the English classroom occurs during guided instruction. This is the time in which "we do it," meaning that teachers and students work together and responsibility is shared. While this can occur as a whole class activity, it is most often realized as needs-based groups of students who meet with the teacher for specific instruction designed to address areas of weakness or future growth. These groups can focus on grammar, mechanics, idea development, comprehension, or any other number of areas in which students need purposeful and explicit instruction. English language learners, in particular, benefit from small group instruction as it is far less intimidating to speak out in front of just a few other students. In a large group, ELLs often tend to sit passively, neither practicing language nor engaging in learning. Guided instruction groups typically last between fifteen and twenty minutes, and teachers can meet with one or two groups per day, depending on the length of the class.

Guided instruction targeted to areas of student need allow teachers to be much more exacting in their instruction. As Fullan, Hill, and Crévola (2006) note, we do not need more prescriptive teaching, but rather more precision in our teaching. This precision will come when we understand the language and literacy development of our students and plan for needs-based interventions.

Collaborative Learning. The most common question we get about guided instruction is "What will the other students do while I meet with four, five, or six students in a small group?" Unfortunately, in too many classrooms this question is left unanswered, and the teacher either leaves students to work independently or abandons guided instruction altogether. Our answer to this question is collaborative learning activities in which students work together in purposeful ways to consolidate their learning. These collaborative learning activities must be directly linked to the purpose of the lesson—the focus—and provide students with opportunities to discuss and engage. It is the time of the lesson in which the teacher says, "You do it together."

There are a number of ways that students can collaborate with one another, including peer response groups, partner reading, book clubs, literature circles, reciprocal teaching, editing conferences, and the like. The goal is that students work side by side and engage with one another, in the absence of the teacher who provides prompts, questions, and clues. Just like the small group guided instruction, this collaborative work provides an environment in which students who are learning English are more comfortable taking the risks that are so vital to learning language. They have significantly increased opportunities to practice language and clarify understanding as they listen to and talk with their peers.

Independent Reading and Writing. The goal of our collective work is skilled readers and writers who complete tasks independently. To that end, students need opportunities to practice and apply what they have learned on their own. Students need to read independently and widely, they need to write for themselves and others, and they need to think about the content they are studying. In some classrooms, students enter and are asked to work independently day after day. It's still far too common for students to enter a classroom and see written on the board, "Read pages 284–301 and answer the questions at the end of the chapter." These classrooms do not work for English language learners (and probably most other students). Without the scaffolding provided through a gradual release of responsibility, English language learners will continue to perform poorly in school, drop out before completing high school, and fail to reach their potential.

Although independent work is a critical step in the learning process, English language learners may need to spend more time in the first three phases of instruction—"I do it," "We do it," and "You do it together"—before they can access and construct grade-level text on their own for extended periods of time. With instruction linked to student performance data and purposeful lessons, students acquire knowledge and language at amazing speeds. As we noted in those many reports we reviewed, it really is the teacher who makes the difference.

Conclusion

Over the past several decades, teachers and researchers have learned a great deal about effective instruction for English language learners. We are no longer in an era of guessing what works. There is not an unlimited range of effective approaches to teaching English language learners. For students to become proficient with the language, to think critically about the content, we must provide instruction in the language and ample opportunities to practice the language. As Dutro and Moran (2003) noted, students must learn English, not just learn *in* English. There are simply too many students who have become protracted at the intermediate levels of language proficiency, failing to progress any further. Each of the four focus chapters in this book highlights specific strategies to move students beyond this threshold level of proficiency to be able to read, write, listen, and speak grade-level academic English:

- *vocabulary knowledge* to use precise and academic terminology
- *grammar skills* to communicate ideas in standard academic English
- *fluency development* to articulate their thoughts easily in a powerful and effectual manner, and to read and write fluently in order to understand
- *comprehension strategies* to make meaning from grade-level texts across genres and content areas

Focusing on vocabulary, grammar, fluency, and comprehension as we will do in the chapters that follow will ensure that we provide students with the skills and knowledge they need in order to use the English language to negotiate their world.

3 Focus on Vocabulary: Getting the Just Right Word

The difference between the right word and almost the right word is the difference between lightning and a lightning bug.

Mark Twain

The research evidence is clear: vocabulary knowledge is directly related to reading comprehension (e.g., August, Carlo, Dressler, & Snow, 2005; Baumann, Kame'enui, & Ash, 2003; Graves, 2006). The National Reading Panel (2000) noted that comprehension is, at least in part, dependent on vocabulary knowledge. Similarly, the Rand study on reading comprehension is filled with references to the role that vocabulary plays in students' meaning making (Snow, 2002). Graves and Watts-Taffe (2002, p. 141) note that the one-hundred-year history of research on vocabulary suggests the following:

- Vocabulary knowledge is one of the best indicators of verbal ability (Sternberg, 1987; Terman, 1916).
- Vocabulary difficulty strongly influences the readability of text (Klare, 1984).
- Teaching the vocabulary of a selection can improve students' comprehension of that selection (Beck el al., 1982).
- Growing up in poverty can seriously restrict the vocabulary children learn before beginning school and make attaining an adequate vocabulary a challenging task (Hart & Risley, 1995).
- Disadvantaged students are likely to have substantially smaller vocabularies than their more advantaged classmates (White, Graves, & Slater, 1990).
- Lack of vocabulary can be a crucial factor underlying the school failure of disadvantaged students (Becker, 1977).

Vacca and Vacca (1999) remind us that there are at least three types of vocabulary—*general, specialized,* and *technical.* General vocabulary consists primarily of words used in everyday language, usually with agreed-upon meanings and definitions. Examples of general vocabulary words include *large, pretty,* and *plumber.* The meaning of these words tends to be consistent across contexts. In contrast, specialized vocabulary acknowledges that words change meaning across disciplines—these words hold multiple meanings in different content areas. For example, the word *bias* has a common meaning—personal and sometimes unreasoned judgment—as well as a more specialized definition in family and consumer sciences—a line diagonal to the grain of a fabric. Finally, there are technical vocabulary words that are specific to a field of study. *Coda* in music, *tectonic plates* in science, *rhombus* in mathematics, and *denouement* in English are all examples of technical vocabulary specific to a content area.

Why Vocabulary Matters for English Language Learners

Adolescent English language learners have an uncanny ability to fool their teachers. Developmentally, they are rapidly approaching adulthood and exhibit all the expected hallmarks of the age group—eager for independence, keen for a debate on matters great and small, and always enthusiastic about the social swirl around them. It is these very behaviors that can fool us into believing that they are more skillful users of the language than they really are. Their need for independence makes them reluctant to seek help, and their adeptness at social discourse can mask their lack of academic language development. They can fly under the radar of English teachers who can be distracted by their students' mastery of social language, only to discover the truth when the first written assignments are turned in. Too often, their command of academic language use, both verbal and written, lags significantly behind their conversational skills. Lack of academic language prevents them from discussing Hamlet's dramatic monologue, writing a persuasive essay, or using rhetorical devices in speech and print. Academic vocabulary extends beyond the generalized vocabulary of everyday speech and print and depends on the development of their specialized and technical vocabulary. As Raquel noted in an interview, "One of the hardest things about reading is the vocabulary. My vocabulary is limited, even in my first language, because I was only fourteen when I came here."

English language learners are further hampered by the rapid increase in the vocabulary load associated with middle and high school course work. Nagy and Anderson (1984) famously reported that by the time they enter high school, students needed to know some 88,500 word *families* (not individual words) in order to read the textbooks and other print materials in their classes. Nagy and Herman (1984) further found that of the 3,000 to 4,000 words learned per year, fewer than 10 percent could be attributed to direct vocabulary instruction. Instead, they found that most of the gains in vocabulary were attributed to acquisition within the context of learning, that is, through reading, writing, thinking, and speaking about concepts. This poses a conundrum for English teachers: students who are English language learners can acquire new vocabulary most effectively when it occurs within the context of learning, yet they are likely to lack the kind of vocabulary needed to read, write, and discuss the very content used during instruction.

This is not a small issue, and there is a good deal of debate on the topic of vocabulary instruction for English language learners. On the one hand, it has been estimated that knowledge of 2,000 to 3,000 words will allow second language learners to understand about 85 percent of a written text (Coady, Magoto, Hubbard, Graney, & Mokhtari, 1993). However, Blachowicz and Fisher (2000) point out that secondary English language learners need to know low-frequency vocabulary to comprehend the academic texts used in school, and that much of this vocabulary is encountered primarily through reading. As Wu (1996) discussed, secondary English language learners are pressed to learn both the content and the language simultaneously. When it comes to vocabulary instruction, it appears that these learners require both direct instruction in core vocabulary and opportunities for wide reading to build background knowledge and acquire low-frequency vocabulary in context.

Vocabulary Instruction

The good news about vocabulary instruction is that it is one of the most researched aspects of literacy. The second article in the first issue of the *School Review of Secondary Education* in 1893 was devoted to the need for sound instructional methods in high school English classes (the first article was on the need for content expertise in teaching). In this article, Wright advised ninth-grade English teachers to "give some attention to suffixes and prefixes, and to the derivation of words" and to "require the defining of new words, to enlarge the pupils [*sic*] vocabulary old words, to make his knowledge accurate" (1893, p. 23). Since that time, vocabulary instruction has remained the focus of literally thousands of research studies. More than a century later, Blachowicz and Fisher (2000) reviewed many of these studies and found that four principles describe the work of effective teachers of vocabulary:

> 1. The effective vocabulary teacher builds a word-rich environment in which students are immersed in words for both incidental and intentional learning.
> 2. The effective vocabulary teacher helps students develop as independent word learners.
> 3. The effective vocabulary teacher uses instructional strategies that not only teach vocabulary effectively but model good word-learning behaviors.
> 4. The effective vocabulary teacher uses assessment that matches the goals of instruction. (2002, p. 7)

To improve vocabulary achievement, as well as overall reading and writing achievement, we suggest that teachers focus on five curricular components. Taken together, these five components are a powerful intervention. In isolation, they are unlikely to significantly improve student achievement. Remember that English language learners need both specific instruction *and* opportunities to develop their word knowledge contextually.

Instructional Strategies for Focusing on Vocabulary

Component 1: Wide Reading

> The man who does not read good books has no advantage over the man who can't read them. (Mark Twain)

The first component is wide reading. Given the research in this area that suggests that time spent reading is one of the ways that students increase their vocabulary knowledge (e.g., Cunningham & Stanovich, 1998; Herman, Anderson, Pearson, & Nagy, 1987; Krashen, 1993), teachers must focus on both Silent Sustained Reading (SSR) and independent reading across content areas. Pilgreen and Krashen (1993) found that SSR had a positive impact on reading comprehension and motivation among high school English language learners. Inspired by these findings, teachers at Hoover High School, where 65 percent of the student body are English language learners, reinvested in a twenty-minute per day Silent Sustained Reading period that the principal noted would provide students with "the opportunity to read" (Fisher, 2004). Every student, teacher, administrator, counselor, health worker, clerical staff—anyone on the campus really—spends twenty minutes every single day of the school year just reading (Ivey & Broaddus, 2001). This initiative

Cooper, M. L. (2000). *Fighting for honor: Japanese Americans and World War II.* New York: Clarion.

Cooper, M. L. (2002). *Remembering Manzanar: Life in a Japanese relocation camp.* New York: Clarion.

Dempster, B. K. (Ed.). (2004). *From our side of the fence: Growing up in America's concentration camps.* San Francisco: Kearny Street Workshop.

Denenberg, B (1999). *The journal of Ben Uchida: Citizen 13559, Mirror Lake Internment Camp.* New York: Scholastic.

Otsuka, J. (2002). *When the emperor was divine.* New York: Anchor.

Sakata, Y. (1992). *The view from within: Japanese American art from the internment camps, 1942–1945.* Los Angeles: Japanese American National Museum.

Tunnell, M. O., & Chilcoat, G. W. (1996). *The children of Topaz: The story of a Japanese-American internment camp based on a classroom diary.* New York: Holiday House.

Uchida, Y. (1984). *Desert exile: The uprooting of a Japanese-American family* (reprint edition). Seattle: University of Washington Press.

Welch, C. A. (2000). *Children of the relocation camps.* Minneapolis, MN: Carolrhoda Books.

Figure 3.1. Independent reading books on Japanese internment camps.

required that the school purchase books that English language learners would and could read. SSR libraries for ELL students should contain a variety of high-interest, low-reading-level books on topics of interest to adolescents. Since much of the fiction written at this level can be somewhat juvenile, older English language learners may be more motivated to read nonfiction.

In addition to the daily practice of SSR, students have time for independent reading in their content area classes, including English (Ivey, 2002). Independent reading during content instruction provides students with access to a wide range of books on the topics they are studying. Figure 3.1 contains a sample of the large number of titles made available by an English teacher for independent student reading during their exploration of World War II and the Japanese internment camps. Their teacher wanted to ensure that she built their background knowledge through wide reading as students in this class were exploring the novel *Snow Falling on Cedars* (Guterson, 1994). As we discussed in Chapter 2, the teacher used a gradual release of responsibility model and read the text aloud, facilitated discussions about the plot, characters, setting, and literary devices, and engaged students in reading related texts. By providing time and materials for students to engage in independent reading related to the unit, students learned technical vocabulary such as *exile, Executive Order 9066, internment, relocation, barracks, Nisei,* and *Issei.* In addition, students gained valuable insight into the historical background of the novel, which takes place nine years after the war is over. Knowledge of this history allowed students to more fully understand the author's use of flashback, mood, and tone, as well as the ability to detect the hostility lying just below the surface of the characters' dialogue. It is important to note that these independent reading books encompass a wide range of reading difficulty and represent a number of genres, including fiction, graphic novels, and informational texts.

Wide Reading and English Language Learners

As noted earlier in the chapter, opportunities for wide reading have been found to be effective in increasing vocabulary knowledge of English language learners, especially as it applies to low-incidence terms and phrases (Krashen, 1993; Zimmerman, 1997). However, merely putting texts in the vicinity of English language learners is not enough. They also need tools to support their reading, especially in dealing with unfamiliar terms. This includes instruction in recognizing and discerning context clues, analyzing word structure, activating prior knowledge, and using dictionaries and other references judiciously.

Teachers can teach students to use contextual analysis as a tool for determining the meaning of unfamiliar vocabulary. There are a variety of context clues, including definition, synonym, antonym, example, and general clues (Baumann, Edwards, Boland, Olejnik, & Kame'enui, 2003). We have provided examples of each, with the target vocabulary underlined and the contextual clue in italics:

- **Definition**: Many <u>Nisei</u>, who were *American-born Japanese,* could not believe they could be sent to internment camps.
- **Synonym**: Kabuo and his wife, Hatsue, were <u>relocated</u> to a camp in the Northwest. They lost their land when they were *put someplace else* for the rest of the war.
- **Antonym**: The island in the novel is a symbol for <u>isolation</u> and the impossibility of living without *connections to other people.*
- **Example**: The president can sign emergency federal orders, *such as* <u>Executive Order 9066</u>, in times of war.
- **General**: <u>Exile</u> was devastating for the people involved because they were *forcibly removed from their homes* and *sent far away* to strange lands.

Although using the context to determine meaning is an invaluable tool, as with any other tool, we must be cautious in its use. In order to make an accurate guess at the meaning of a particular word, the reader must first understand a significant amount of the surrounding text. English language learners often do not have an adequate vocabulary to make sense of one particular word in their reading. In many cases, there is not enough information in a single sentence to help students figure out the meaning of the unknown word. Consider the sentence below:

> Although the students were exuberant, the teacher was dispirited.

In this sentence, if the students recognize *although* as a word that signals the opposite, they may understand that *exuberant* and *dispirited* are antonyms. However, they still must know the meaning of one or the other of those words in order to determine the meaning of the other. It is possible that the surrounding sentences provide enough context for students to deduce the meaning. So when we teach them to use context clues, we must be sure that their understanding of "context" goes beyond the immediate sentence, extending into what they have read before as well as the text that follows. As Allen (1999) explains:

> If the context is specific enough for students to recognize, define, or make sense of the word and if there is enough information to allow students to connect the word to their background knowledge, no additional instruction is necessary. If not, the word or concept requires teacher mediation. (p. 18)

Students also must learn to use dictionaries—electronic or print bilingual dictionaries can be particularly helpful (e.g., Knight, 1994), though we do not recommend reliance on them. Some studies of extensive use of these reference materials did not yield appreciable results in reading comprehension (J. N. Davis, 1989; Laufer & Hadar, 1997). Since stopping to look up words in the dictionary slows reading quite a bit, students should be taught to use this reference tool only when it becomes apparent that the missing word is critical to understanding the passage.

Component 2: Teacher Read-Alouds

> A word is dead when it is said, some say. I say it just begins to live that day. (Emily Dickinson)

A second component of a vocabulary initiative focuses on teachers reading aloud to students. While the link between teacher read-alouds and vocabulary learning is clear (e.g., Elley, 1989; Penno, Wilkinson, & Moore, 2002; Schippert, 2005), motivating high school teachers to read aloud to their students on a daily basis is difficult. From a student perspective, the read-aloud is a helpful way to learn content and vocabulary. As Ivey (2003) noted, "The teacher makes it more explainable" with read-alouds (p. 812).

Read-alouds serve three purposes for secondary English language learners. First, they provide the teacher with an opportunity to build essential background knowledge—widely regarded as a fundamental principle for effective education of second language learners (Hill & Flynn, 2006). Second, read-alouds allow teachers to model fluent oral reading of texts, including pronunciation of unfamiliar words. Third, teachers who read aloud are able to "think aloud," a process of elaboration used to clarify, make connections, and model comprehension strategies, as is discussed further in Chapter 6.

Teacher Read-Alouds and English Language Learners

As with wide reading, read-alouds are used in English classrooms to build background knowledge, although their functions differ. While wide reading is used to extend student knowledge of content, read-alouds are effective for introducing concepts. Ivey and Broaddus (2001) found that the middle school students in their study identified teacher read-alouds as the preferred way to learn new content. This is especially important in light of what we know about vocabulary development—that it is learned in context, and that it requires repeated exposures.

To ensure that teacher read-alouds are of high quality and improve student achievement, we recommend the following practices identified by Fisher, Flood, Lapp, and Frey (2004):

1. Select books that are appropriate to students' interests and match their developmental, emotional, and social levels.
2. Preview and practice the selection.
3. Establish a clear purpose for the read-aloud.
4. Model fluent oral reading while reading the text.
5. Be animated and use expression.
6. Stop periodically and thoughtfully question the students to focus them on specifics of the text.
7. Make connections to independent reading and writing.

These read-aloud practices are consistent with the research on effective practices for making content comprehensible to adolescent English language learners. Indeed, the associations are remarkable. Free-

Jabberwocky

'Twas brillig, and the slithy toves
Did gyre and gimble in the wabe:
All mimsy were the borogoves,
And the mome raths outgrabe.

"Beware the Jabberwock, my son!
The jaws that bite, the claws that catch!
Beware the Jubjub bird, and shun
The frumious Bandersnatch!"

He took his vorpal sword in hand:
Long time the manxome foe he sought—
So rested he by the Tumtum tree,
And stood awhile in thought.

And, as in uffish thought he stood,
The Jabberwock, with eyes of flame,
Came whiffling through the tulgey wood,
And burbled as it came!

One, two! One, two! And through and through
The vorpal blade went snicker-snack!
He left it dead, and with its head
He went galumphing back.

"And, has thou slain the Jabberwock?
Come to my arms, my beamish boy!
O frabjous day! Callooh! Callay!'
He chortled in his joy.

'Twas brillig, and the slithy toves
Did gyre and gimble in the wabe;
All mimsy were the borogoves,
And the mome raths outgrabe.

Figure 3.2. "Jabberwocky" by Lewis Carroll from *Through the Looking-Glass and What Alice Found There*, 1872.

man and Freeman's (2002) review of language strategies included using visuals, body language, and pausing frequently. In addition, they advise checking for understanding often and inviting students to participate in summarizing main ideas.

Consider, for example, tenth-grade English teacher Michelle Herzog's read-aloud of Lewis Carroll's "Jabberwocky" (see Figure 3.2). She discussed the author's use of nonsense words and how not knowing the words makes reading confusing. As she read this poem aloud to her students, Ms. Herzog shared her thinking with them. She modeled the use of context clues to figure out what the author was saying. As she read the first two lines, she asked aloud, "What did the toves do in the wabe?" She then reread the lines and used the context clues to answer herself, "Oh, they gyre and gimbled." She shared her use of context clues, saying, "I don't really know the words *gyre* or *gimble*, but I know that I can use context clues to figure out what the author is saying. I know that where the words are in a sentence matters and that I can use that information to figure out the answers to some of these questions."

A more traditional read-aloud designed to build students' vocabulary knowledge was conducted by eighth-grade English teacher Mike Bishop. During his read-aloud of Amy Tan's short story "Rules of the Game," which became part of the work of fiction known as *The Joy Luck Club* (1989), Mr. Bishop models vocabulary thinking and learning strategies for his students so that they can use these strategies on their own during independent reading. In addition to knowing that read-alouds provide students with incidental vocabulary development, Mr. Bishop knows that he can teach his students, through modeling, how to solve unknown words. For example, at one point in the short story, Mr. Bishop reads, "My mother imparted her daily truths so she could help my older brothers and me rise above our circumstances." After reading that sentence, Mr. Bishop paused and explained his thinking about some of the words to his students. Part of the conversation went like this:

> *Imparted*, that's an interesting word. I'll use some context clues to figure that out. So, she says that mom does something with truths so that we can rise or get better lives. I think I'll try some substitutions to see if they work. I'm thinking about *shared*, my mother shared her daily truths. That fits with the context. *Tell* or *told* might also work, my mother told her daily truths. Yeah, I think that *imparted* is to tell something or share something. We already know the harder word, circumstances, as we've used it a lot to describe the way that things are. So, this means that mom told things to help the kids change the way that things were in their lives.

Component 3: Content Vocabulary Instruction

When ideas fail, words come in very handy. (Goethe)

Content-specific vocabulary is critical in every discipline. In the secondary English classroom, we need for students to understand a wide range of words such as *genre*, *personification*, *simile*, and *conflict*. Teachers should regularly use a number of defensible instructional strategies to engage students in vocabulary learning, including vocabulary journals, vocabulary role-play, word sorts, semantic feature analysis charts, list/group/label, semantic mapping, vocabulary cards, barrier games, concept ladders, and word walls (e.g., Brassell & Flood, 2004).

Content Vocabulary Instruction and English Language Learners

As Dutro and Moran (2003) describe, brick words are the content vocabulary of instruction, such as *simile* and *personification*, while mortar words link these concepts together into cohesive sentences, like *after, went,* and *affect*. English language learners are challenged to learn both simultaneously, and benefit from direct instruction that considers both (see the next section for instruction in the "mortar words" of general academic vocabulary).

For example, a teacher may use vocabulary role-play, a strategy that allows students to act out new vocabulary. Consider the humanities teacher who wanted to target vocabulary words such as *inflation*. In this class, students can perform their understanding of inflation by miming themselves getting wider and bigger and then handing each other more and more money.

Since students also need to see how vocabulary concepts relate to one another, they can keep vocabulary journals for the key content terms of the class to add new information throughout the semester. Table 3.1 contains entries from a vocabulary journal on archetypes. As they read new books, they add information about major characters.

It is important to note that teachers should use a range of instructional strategies for content vocabulary study such that students do not become bored with vocabulary learning. Understanding the instructional strategies useful in content vocabulary learning is important, but so is word selection. In different classes, for example, different terms are often being taught. An eleventh-grade English teacher said to us, "I can't guarantee that all of my students will have the same content vocabulary knowledge—they know different words based on who their teacher was—so I teach all of the students all the words, even if some of them already know them."

To remedy this situation, to create some agreements, and to ensure that students have access to instruction in key terms, teachers in each course should identify key terms that students should know. To select these key terms, teachers should ask themselves and others specific questions about the word, including:

- **Representative**: Is the concept represented by the word critical to understanding the text?

Table 3.1. Vocabulary Journal Entries about Archetypes

Terms	Meaning	Examples in Film and TV	Examples in Literature
The Self-Doubting Hero	A heroic figure who questions his role and purpose	Harry Potter, Neo (*The Matrix*)	Hamlet, Manny Hernandez (*Parrot in the Oven*)
The Trickster	Clever; disobeys rules	Bugs Bunny, Roadrunner, Captain Jack Sparrow	The Gravediggers (*Hamlet*), Jabuti (*Jabuti the Tortoise*)
The Magician	Wise mentor who advises hero and draws on mysterious strengths	Obi-Wan Kenobe (*Star Wars*), Dumbledore (*Harry Potter*)	Merlin (*A Connecticut Yankee in King Arthur's Court*), Melquíades (*One Hundred Years of Solitude*)
The Great Mother	A strong, wise, and all-protecting female	Fairy Godmother (*Cinderella*)	Sophia (*The Color Purple*), Ultima (*Bless Me, Ultima*), Lindo Jong (*Joy Luck Club*)
The Eternal Boy	An adolescent or young adult male who resists adult responsibility	Peter Pan	Aureliano Segundo (*One Hundred Years of Solitude*)
The Savior	The rescuer—often condemned for enlightened view	Luke Skywalker (*Star Wars*)	Prometheus, Atticus Finch (*To Kill a Mockingbird*)
The Outcast	Marginalized by a society (can be voluntary)	Eric Cartman ("South Park"), Eminem	Simon (*Lord of the Flies*), Holden Caulfield (*Catcher in the Rye*), Estha (*The God of Small Things*)
The Powerful Villain	Battles the hero; uses power to harm others	Darth Vader (*Star Wars*), Lord Voldemort (*Harry Potter*)	Agamemnon (*The Odyssey*), The Red Queen (*Through the Looking Glass*)

- **Repeatability**: Will the word be used again during the school year?
- **Transportability**: Will the word be used in other subject areas?
- **Contextual analysis**: Is there a rich context that provides sufficient clues for students to determine the word meaning?
- **Structural analysis**: Can students use structural analysis to determine the word meaning?

- **Cognitive load**: How many words can students be expected to learn at one time?

These conversations will result in the identification of specific terms that students need to know in each of their English classes. Of course, teachers can add terms to these minimum expectations and can teach the vocabulary terms in a variety of ways. The point is that students will learn the vocabulary of the discipline through evidence-based instructional practices and not be expected to simply absorb these concepts and terms from being in the classroom.

An example of this comes from a team of ninth-grade teachers who wanted their students to develop vocabulary knowledge related to transitions. After examining the writing of their students, they knew that their students found transitions to be difficult and often left them out entirely, producing disjointed, awkward text. This group of teachers used a word list to help students understand the types of transitions necessary in good writing (see Table 3.2). They created a word wall containing these words and regularly reviewed the list. They also highlighted, during their read-alouds, when authors used words from their list. Over time, students started to notice the terms in their reading and began incorporating them into their writing. Again, the focus on vocabulary—both content specific and general academic—necessary to engage in classroom discourse was an important factor in the literacy development of English language learners.

Component 4: Academic Word Study

> "When I use a word," Humpty Dumpty said, in a rather scornful tone, "it means just what I chose it to mean—neither more nor less."
>
> "The question is," said Alice, "whether you can make words mean so many different things." (Lewis Carroll, *Through the Looking Glass and What Alice Found There*)

As Lewis Carroll reminds us, there are a significant number of words that mean different things in different contexts. Although it may not be that one can make the word mean anything, some words certainly do have a lot of different meanings. Understanding the word *run*, for example, is dependent on determining the context in which it is used. Imagine how many times a day a teacher could use run—*run* to the office, *run* this off, *run* for office, *run* the program, *run* in my pantyhose, *runny* nose, I've got the *runs*, and so on. These words are especially vexing for English language learners who may know a few ways that words can be used, but who may be overwhelmed with the sixty-nine definitions for *run* found in the dictionary.

Table 3.2. Transition Words Categorized by Function

Addition	■ also ■ and ■ besides ■ furthermore ■ in addition	■ indeed ■ in fact ■ moreover ■ so too
Example	■ after all ■ as an illustration ■ for example	■ for instance ■ specifically ■ to take a case in point
Comparison	■ along the same lines ■ in the same way	■ likewise ■ similarly
Contrast	■ although ■ but ■ by contrast ■ conversely ■ despite the fact ■ even though ■ however ■ in contrast	■ nevertheless ■ nonetheless ■ on the contrary ■ on the other hand ■ regardless ■ whereas ■ while yet
Cause and effect	■ accordingly ■ as a result ■ consequently ■ hence ■ since	■ so ■ then ■ therefore ■ thus
Concession	■ admittedly ■ although it is true ■ granted	■ naturally ■ of course ■ to be sure
Conclusion	■ as a result ■ consequently ■ hence ■ in conclusion ■ in short	■ in sum ■ therefore ■ thus ■ to sum up ■ to summarize

Source: From *"They Say/I Say": The Moves That Matter in Academic Writing* by Gerald Graff & Cathy Birkenstein.

Academic Word Study and English Language Learners

Like the "brick" words of content vocabulary instruction, these "mortar" words play an essential role in understanding text. Unfortunately, these are the very words that many secondary teachers overlook because it is expected that students will have acquired them already. This is not the case for many middle and high school English language learners, and their textbooks rarely provide contextual clues about the meaning of such words (Rothenberg & Fisher, 2007).

However, the opportunity to offer academic vocabulary instruction is there, provided we are aware of its importance. It is easy to imagine that a student comes into contact with the term *prime* and a variety of words associated with prime, such as *primary*, *primarily*, *prime meridian*, and *primacy*, a number of times during the school year. The student's understanding of the term is further complicated by the way in which the term is specifically used in mathematics versus the English classroom.

Although most teachers are skilled at providing vocabulary instruction in content-specific words, attention to multiple meaning, specialized, and academic vocabulary is often limited. Consider the following example from a core reading text:

> Catherine the great, a minor aristocrat from Germany, became Empress of Russia when her husband Peter, the grandson of Peter the Great, was killed.

If you can, ignore the number of appositives for a minute. On which word would English language learners benefit from instruction? Most teachers unfamiliar with specialized vocabulary or the needs of English language learners would focus on the word *aristocrat*. We would argue, however, that if there were only time for attention to one word from this paragraph, it should be *minor*. English language learners might know one meaning for the word *minor*, but they are unlikely to understand that this word could be used correctly in this sentence to mean either "underage" or "not important." Note that in this case, context clues don't help with figuring out which use the author intended—they both make sense.

In an effort to identify academic words that the students need to know, Coxhead (2000) analyzed 3.5 million running words of written academic text. She excluded the 2,000 words of "greatest service in English" identified by West (1953), such as *the*, *however*, and *order*. The resulting list of 570 word families accounts for a significant portion of specialized words found in content area texts. This list, called the Academic Word List (AWL), can be found at http://www.vuw.ac.nz/lals/research/awl/. It is important to note that academic vocabulary is an area of need for both English language learners and standard English learners.

English teachers can use the Academic Word List in a number of ways. Some teachers ask students to create Frayer model vocabulary word cards, which encourage learners to think about new vocabulary through definition, examples, contrasts, and visual representations. One student developed a vocabulary card in which she used *minor* as a contrastive to the word *significant* and then drew a key to remind herself that something significant can be the key to understanding (see Figure 3.3). Other teachers add the academic vocabulary terms to note-taking guides and help students think through the various uses of the term, deciding which use works best for the content at hand.

Component 5: Words of the Week

> "My spelling is Wobbly. It's good spelling, but it Wobbles, and the letters get in the wrong places." (Winnie the Pooh)

The final component of a vocabulary learning initiative centers on students learning transportable word parts. English language learners often have a difficult time making an educated guess about an unknown word because they do not understand the parts of the word. There is evidence for studying one word per day (e.g., Graves & Watts-Taffe, 2002; Stahl, 1998) as well as evidence for students learning common affixes (e.g., Carnine & Carnine, 2004; White, Power, & White, 1989). This word-learning strategy is also useful for standard English learners who often use simple vocabulary and slang rather than academic terms.

Word Parts and English Language Learners

Just as content and academic vocabulary serve as the bricks and mortar of sentences, word parts can be described as the ingredients necessary to make those materials. Word parts, especially affixes and roots, are vital for English language learners who need the tools to deconstruct unfamiliar words independently.

Given the language learning needs of many English language learners, we recommend a "Words of the Week" (WOW) program. For each week of the school year, a specific prefix, suffix, or root is identified. Five words containing the identified prefix, suffix, or root are then selected. The purpose is not only to instruct students on the meanings and uses of the listed words, but also to develop a schema for under-

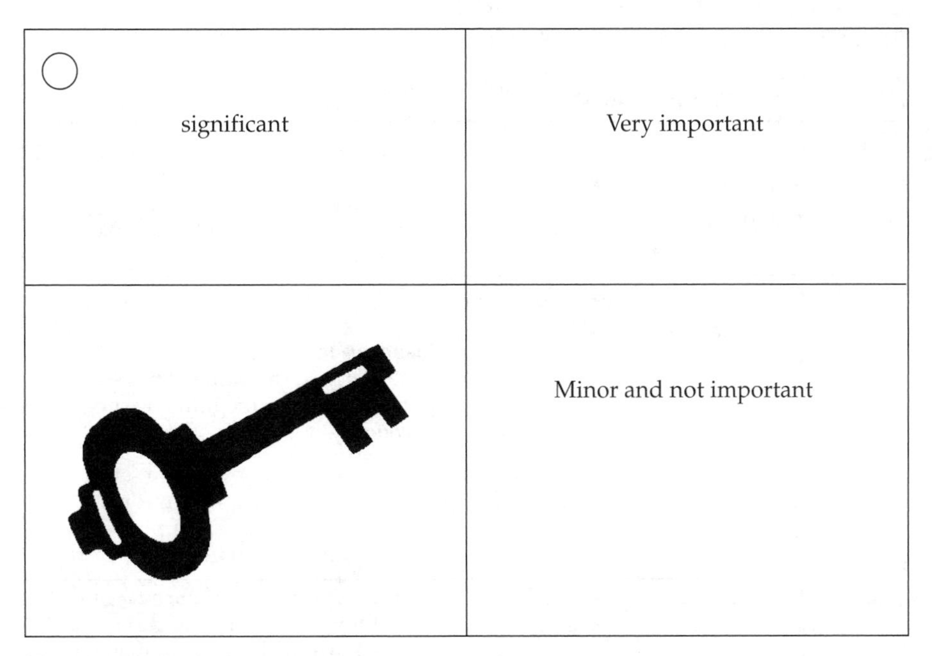

Figure 3.3. Frayer vocabulary card model.

standing the relationship between words with similar word parts. Consider this list: *malodorous, malcontent, malaria, malevolent,* and *malicious.* Besides learning these words, students also learn that *mal-* in a word means "bad." Spanish speakers, recognizing that *mal* means "bad" in Spanish, can connect their knowledge of their own language to help deconstruct these words. And since many affixes and roots are Latin-based, they can use their primary language to unlock the code of countless academic words. Therefore, a later encounter with the word *maladaptive* becomes a bit easier. Part of the power in this program is that every teacher in a school can use, teach, and reinforce the WOW words.

To increase the contexts in which students might find the words, several routes can be identified. Hoover High School used WOW to improve vocabulary and found a number of ways to increase students' interactions with the words. First, the student government class was asked to incorporate the five words of the week on the electronic marquis that announces all of the events on the campus. Second, Lulu Gallegos, a front office clerical staff member, volunteered to write a humorous sentence each week containing the five words and place it in the school bulletin (see Table 3.3 for examples).

Table 3.3. Words of the Week Sentences

Week	Words of the Week	Sentence of the Week
2	■ audience ■ audition ■ auditor ■ auditory ■ inaudible	If you are granted an audience with the tax auditor, speak as though you are at an audition for he has an auditory problem and your voice may be inaudible.
3	■ affluent ■ fluctuate ■ fluent ■ fluorescent ■ influence	Under the harsh glare of fluorescent lighting, the affluent woman's facial features looked strangely fluent as she watched the value of her stock fluctuate under the influence of the economy.
4	■ primarily ■ primate ■ primer ■ primitive ■ primeval	In the forest primeval once sat a primate in his primitive hut made primarily of tree bark, applying mud to the walls as though it were primer.
5	■ assimilate ■ facsimile ■ simultaneously ■ simile ■ simulate	Send my brother and me a facsimile and though we will read it simultaneously we will each assimilate the information at a different pace.
6	■ construct ■ destructive ■ infrastructure ■ instrumental ■ obstruction	In order to construct a destructive infrastructure, it is instrumental to eliminate all obstructions.
7	■ intuition ■ tutelage ■ tutor ■ tutorial ■ tuition	Although Larry paid a very small tuition for Moe's tutelage, his intuition told him using a computer tutorial would be less painful than the blows to the head which his current tutor used to emphasize each point.

Third, students were invited to perform raps with the Words of the Week in the back quad area every Thursday. The first rap ever performed using WOW was written and performed by Sashay. It reads:

> I'm *fluent* on the mic because I flow with confidence. When I spit, I'm *fluorescent*, homie, don't get me twisted. Inside and out, I *fluctuate* on the stage just to hype the crowd. I know you love the way I bling when I move about. My good *influence* keeps me *affluent*, so the money neva run out. As long as I'm doing what I'm doing, I'll be famous in a big white house.

Fourth, on Thursdays during passing periods and lunch, the administrative team walks through the school, pausing to ask students the meanings of the Words of the Week. When a student answers correctly, he or she is given a student store credit worth ten cents.

Keep in mind that the goal of Words of the Week is not for students to memorize a list of specific words, but rather to develop skills to make educated guesses about unfamiliar words while they are reading. In doing so, they are more likely to be able to use context clues, their background knowledge, and motivation to read for understanding—the goal of vocabulary learning.

Despite this goal, it is interesting to note how many times students incorporate the Words of the Week into their writing. Raquel, now a college sophomore, told us, "I love those words! I use them now in my essays." Fernando, a tenth grader, wrote the following note to his ROTC instructor using words that had been the focus the previous school year:

> Hello Colonel,
> Have a Merry Christmas and a Happy New Year. Stay out of trouble during the holidays. Don't go around fracturing people's fragile hearts with your fractious behavior.
> Fernando

Leadership in English

Supporting Schoolwide Efforts in Wide Reading

One of the ways that English teachers can improve the vocabulary knowledge of their students is through advocating that all content area teachers provide students with an opportunity for independent reading. For example, a science teacher known for his focus on standards and use of the standards-aligned textbook noted that the introduction of Silent Sustained Reading and independent reading had positively impacted his students' understanding of the content. As he said, "I was doing all the work. There I was, telling them to read and then telling them what the book said. I still use the text[book], but now I have students spend part of the period reading from a wide collection of books and magazine articles. They can choose something to read and they all end up with some interesting connections and facts that others don't know. This means we have amazing conversations about the standards. I'm still teaching the standards and always will. Inviting students to read other texts moves the responsibility from me to them."

Supporting Schoolwide Efforts in Read-Alouds

There are a number of resources for teacher read-alouds, including material from *Read It Aloud! Using Literature in the Secondary Content*

Classroom (Richardson, 2000), *Read All about It! Great Read-Aloud Stories, Poems, and Newspaper Pieces for Preteens and Teens* (Trelease, 1993), and a journal article titled "Not Just for the Primary Grades: A Bibliography of Picture Books for Secondary Content Teachers" (Carr, Buchanan, Wentz, Weiss, & Brant, 2001). In some schools, the librarian uses some of the book funds to purchase materials for teachers to read aloud to their classes. For example, as part of their work on improving vocabulary through read-alouds at Hoover High, a family and consumer sciences teacher who wanted books about eating disorders got *Hunger Point: A Novel* (Medoff, 2001), a physics teacher who wanted to talk about relationship violence got *Dreamland* (Dessen, 2000), and an English teacher who wanted an epic journey with a twist got the graphic novel *Bone* (J. Smith, 1994).

With support from an English teacher, a physics teacher identified a number of read-alouds for her unit of study titled "Motion and Forces." Among the collection of newspaper and magazine articles, the following supplemental readings can be found:

- Allan, T. (2001). *Isaac Newton*. Portsmouth, NH: Heinemann.
- Henderson, C., & Smith, A. (2001). *The Usborne Internet-linked library of science: Energy, forces, and motion*. London: Usborne.
- Lafferty, P. (1999). *Eyewitness: Force and motion*. DK Children.
- Twist, C. (2005). *Force and motion*. New York: Bearport.
- White, M. (1999). *Isaac Newton: Discovering laws that govern the universe*. Woodbridge, CT: Blackbirch Press.

The first standard in physics requires that students are familiar with Newton's laws that predict the motion of most objects. As students listen to the teacher read these books aloud, they become familiar with the vocabulary that scientists use to discuss Newton's laws, such as constant speed and average speed, acceleration, gravity, force, speed, friction, and vectors.

Supporting Schoolwide Efforts in Content and Academic Vocabulary Instruction

Although most content teachers will readily cite vocabulary as an important part of their course, many will also add that their instruction is limited to listing words, perhaps with requirements to write definitions. Unfortunately, the end result is a long list (up to fifty words!) assigned on a worksheet, few of which are mastered beyond the next test. Again, the English department can serve as the catalyst by helping each of the other content areas select and focus on content vocabulary. The guidelines for selecting vocabulary—representative, repeatability, transportability, contextual analysis, structural analysis, and cognitive load—can be useful in dialoguing with colleagues about the number and types of words selected for each unit. Once agreed, these words can become a part of the pacing guides developed by course-alike groups. Another useful academic word list has been developed by Marzano and Pickering (2005). It contains nearly eight hundred words and is organized by eleven content areas.

The vocabulary lists developed by each department can serve a use beyond the course, because these lists can be provided to all the teachers in the grade level. Teachers who know the vocabulary their colleagues are teaching can take the opportunity to make connections as they arise. For example, a tenth-grade history teacher used *absolute* and *relative location* in teaching about geography, while a mathematics colleague drew an analogy to graphing on the x- and y-axis in an algebra unit.

The goal of the academic word study is to develop students' understanding of the multiple ways that words can be used. As a ninth-grade English teacher commented, "It doesn't do much good to know *photosynthesis* if you do not know how to use *acquire, create, environment, expand,* and such. In fact, I'm not sure that they really can get photosynthesis if they don't know the other words that go along with it. Photosynthesis requires that students understand things like acquiring carbon dioxide and water, how the environment impacts plants, how plants create oxygen, and leaves expand in the process gaining mass, and so on. I guess I've learned that knowing a content word requires knowing a lot of academic language."

Supporting Schoolwide Efforts with Words of the Week

Although content teachers are open to content vocabulary instruction, they may be more resistant to teaching words not directly related to their units of instruction. English teachers can assist their content colleagues by providing information about the usefulness of word parts instruction on getting at the "SAT words" that their students will be required to master. In addition, English teachers can take a leadership role in developing and disseminating the Words of the Week lists, along with suggestions on how these words might be easily incorporated into the discourse of various content areas. We've overheard *malodorous* being used by physical education teachers to describe locker rooms and the word *draconian* mentioned more than once in the counseling center! Finally, we recommend that the initial instruction for WOW occur in the

English classroom, where teachers can delve into word origins, cognates, and uses. This is an excellent place for students to create vocabulary word cards and engage in other instructional strategies such as semantic maps and vocabulary journals.

Conclusion

Consider Hatch and Brown's (1995) steps required for English language learners to acquire new vocabulary:

1. The words are used in multiple sources.
2. They are accompanied by visual and auditory cues for remembering the words.
3. The definitions of the words are taught as well.
4. Mnemonic connections are made to ensure retention of the words.
5. Learners have multiple opportunities to use the words in speaking, listening, reading, and writing.

The strategies in this chapter offer a template for providing multiple opportunities for English language learners to interact with content and academic vocabulary throughout the school year and across the day. Keep in mind that we do not recommend a piecemeal approach, but rather a cohesive and systematic plan for vocabulary development. English teachers can assume a leadership position at the school for leading discussions on the need for vocabulary instruction and to model how it can be accomplished more effectively.

4 Focus on Grammar: "It Is Blue?"

I never made a mistake in grammar but one in my life and as soon as I done it I seen it.

Carl Sandburg

Just say the word in most classrooms—*grammar*—and students start to moan. Sadly, there are many students who find the careful examination of the rules of our language exceptionally boring. That may be because of the way grammar was historically taught—decontextualized and through rote memorization. It also may be because students do not see the utility of grammar lessons. Having said that, we know that grammar is critical in order for students to understand the language. Without agreed upon structures and rules, speakers and writers would have a very difficult time communicating. Language is more than random words put together, and verb tense, punctuation, pronouns, and such guide our understanding of the message. As Truss (2004) notes, there is a significant difference between "eats, shoots, and leaves" and "eats shoots and leaves." In other words, comprehension is impacted when students do not understand the rules that govern language use.

In this chapter, we define grammar, explore the reasons that grammar instruction is important for English language learners, consider the ways in which students learn grammar, and focus on quality grammar instruction.

What Is Grammar?

Traditionally, grammar instruction focused on morphology and syntax. Students were required to learn word structure (morphology), a branch of linguistics that concentrates on the ways in which words are related to one another. For example, fluent readers and writers know that *house* is to *houses* as *bird* is to *birds*—they have generalized the word knowledge or morphology of the *-s* ending in English. Students also need to know how words can be combined to form phrases and sentences, which we call syntax. These syntactic rules or "patterned relations" govern the way we can combine words to form phrases and sentences.

For example, fluent users of English understand that the verb form "to be" changes and is the most complex irregular verb in the language. Fluent language learners understand the differences between the following uses of the form:

- I *am* tired.
- I will *be* tired after running.
- Boys will *be* boys.
- Cats *are* felines.

Contemporary grammar adds phonetics, phonology, semantics, and pragmatics to the study of morphology and syntax. Figure 4.1 contains a definition of each of these components of linguistic study. Importantly, grammar has always been a part of the English classroom. However, as Gribbin (2005) notes, "A persistent question throughout the years is to teach grammar or not to teach, along with how much to teach and when" (p. 17). Figure 4.2 lists ten myths about grammar and grammar instruction that Larsen-Freeman (1997) debunks.

Why Is Grammar Important for English Language Learners?

> Ignorant people think it is the noise which fighting cats make that is so aggravating, but it ain't so; it is the sickening grammar that they use. (Mark Twain)

As Mark Twain noted in his characteristically pointed way, incorrect grammar makes one sound ignorant. Understanding this has led many teachers, as well as educational publishers, to focus on the discrete rules of grammar. As a result, many English language learners have memorized the rules for using the English language but do not apply them with consistency and accuracy. As Scarcella (2003) noted, "Knowledge of grammar without the ability to apply it is useless" (p. 61).

But why is grammar instruction critical for English language learners? As Jago (2002), Samway (2006), and others have noted, all students, including English language learners, must receive grammar instruction if they are to perform in academic settings. Learning and understanding grammar facilitates English language development. When students begin to master the rules of the language, they increase their use of vocabulary, become more fluent, read with increased understanding, and write in more precise and interesting ways (Doughty, 1991; Fisher & Frey, 2003; Lightbrown, 1998; Lucas, 2005).

In the past, theorists held that English language learners would naturally acquire the rules of the language (e.g., Krashen, 1981). We

Phonetics: The study of the sounds of speech, especially in physically producing and perceiving the sounds accurately. Physiology and anatomy play a role in phonetics, and it is a necessary component of producing and understanding spoken words. Phonetics involves all the speech sounds that can be produced by humans, including those that are not featured in the focus language. There are more than 100 phonemes (smallest units of speech) in the collective human languages; phonetics involves all of them.

Phonology: The study of how the rules of sound are organized in a focus language (e.g., changes in pronunciation of *r*-controlled vowels in English). Phonology concerns itself with the phonemes of a particular language, such as the approximately 44-46 phonemes of English. As with phonetics, phonological knowledge is essential to understanding and producing comprehensible speech.

Morphology: The study of the rules that govern units of meaning in a language, especially within word structures. Prefixes, suffixes, and roots are all aspects of morphology. *Bird, house*, and *dog* are all free morphemes, meaning that they are the smallest units of meaning and cannot be further parsed. Bound morphemes such as *re-, -s,* and *-tion* also carry a meaning that cannot be reduced. An English language user applies morphological knowledge to understand the difference between *bird* and *birds* as well as the conceptual relationship between these terms.

Semantics: The study of meaning across words, phrases, sentences, and passages. For instance, semantics is used by a language learner to understand the differences and conceptual relationships between *birds, birdhouses, bird dogs*, and *bird walk.*

Syntax: The study of the grammatical rules that govern a language. This includes the study of parts of speech, such as nouns, verbs, and adjectives. All languages possess syntactic structures, although the rules for each vary.

Pragmatics: The study of the relationship between the meaning and the messenger, often considered to be the social aspect of language. Any message must be considered within the context in which it is delivered, and pragmatics is applied by a language learner to understand when to say something and how to say it so that it is interpreted accurately. For example, pragmatics is used to understand the language differences between greeting the school principal and greeting your best friend.

Figure 4.1. Components of linguistics.

know that there are certainly students for whom this generalization is true. However, we now know that there are significant numbers of English language learners who have not progressed beyond intermediate levels of fluency and proficiency because they have not mastered the conventions of the language. This is especially true for the "generation 1.5 students" we introduced in Chapter 1. These students simply do not notice the errors they make and will not learn standard English from interacting with peers, listening to teachers or other adults talk, reading books, or writing in journals (Scarcella & Rumberger, 2000). They

1. Grammar is acquired naturally; it need not be taught.
2. Grammar is a collection of meaningless forms.
3. Grammar consists of arbitrary rules.
4. Grammar is boring.
5. Students have different learning styles. Not all students can learn grammar.
6. Grammar structures are learned one at a time.
7. Grammar has to do only with sentence-level and subsentence-level phenomena.
8. Grammar and vocabulary are areas of knowledge. Reading, writing, speaking, and listening are the four skills.
9. Grammars provide the rules/explanations for all the structures in a language.
10. "I don't know enough to teach grammar."

Figure 4.2. Myths concerning the teaching of grammar. *Source*: Adapted from "Grammar and Its Teaching: Challenging the Myths," by Diane Larsen-Freeman, *Eric Digest*, ED406829 97. Retrieved from http://www.ericdigests.org/1997-4/grammar.htm.

need and deserve a focused approach to grammar instruction that engages, rather than bores, them.

Why Is Grammar Important for Standard English Learners?

Focused grammar instruction is also critical for standard English learners, who possess day-to-day vocabulary and are able to communicate on any number of topics, yet lack proficiency with the academic language required in school. Some ethnolinguists view African American Vernacular English (AAVE) as a language in its own right, derived from the languages of the Niger-Congo region of Africa from which the majority of the enslaved Africans were taken. Analysis of AAVE reveals rules of pronunciation and grammar that are consistent with those of the Niger-Congo languages, suggesting that the early slaves superimposed the English lexicon over the grammatical structures of their native languages (LeMoine, 2006). In AAVE, for instance, there are typically no consonant clusters but rather a consonant-vowel-consonant pattern. So *desk* is pronounced (and thus written) *des*, and *test* becomes *tes*. The *s* is not used as a possessive marker, so *my friend's book* becomes *my friend book*. Neither is *s* used as a plural marker when there is a numerical marker in the same sentence—*50 cents* is expressed as *50 cent*. And verb conjugation is regularized such that students will write *I was* just as they will write *you was*. (This pattern is also true of Hawaiian English). Use of pronouns also follows a regular pattern, forming the reflexive pronoun from the possessive—*myself* comes from the possessive *my*, just as *hisself* comes from *his* (LeMoine, 2006).

An additive approach to teaching grammar to standard English learners is through contrastive analysis. Students can learn standard academic English as they write the same piece of text in different voices, analyzing how the same ideas are expressed in both AAVE and in academic English. They can use graphic organizers to examine the similarities and differences in the structure of their home language and the language of school. And when teachers are aware of these similarities and differences, they can highlight and discuss them as they teach.

How Do Students Learn Grammar?

From the outset, we should acknowledge that we do not advocate traditional or decontextualized grammar instruction (i.e., diagramming, fill-in-the-blank worksheets). In their analysis of the effectiveness of formal grammar instruction, Andrews et al. (2006) noted that there was little evidence to support this approach. They noted that sentence combining, which is discussed later in this chapter, was much more effective than formal grammar instruction such as rote memorization of rules and completing skill worksheets. Similarly, Feng and Powers (2005) noted that the use of students' writing as the fodder for grammar lessons resulted in increased knowledge and skills. Table 4.1 provides a comparison between historical approaches to grammar instruction and those we understand to be effective today.

Table 4.2 provides a graphic representation of the process learners must experience to develop grammatical knowledge. This graphic

Table 4.1. Comparing Approaches to Grammar Instruction

Historical Approaches	Current Approaches
■ Sentence diagramming ■ Memorizing definitions of grammar terms ■ Identifying parts of speech ■ Teaching grammar to the whole class ■ Substitution drills ■ Translation ■ Using a grammatical syllabus to determine when to teach a specific structure	■ Using student writing as fodder for instruction ■ Varying instruction based on student need ■ Using instructional strategies that are flexibly applied to a variety of grammar structures and rules

Source: Adapted from *Accelerating Academic English: A Focus on the English Learner*, by R. Scarcella, 2003 (Oakland, CA: Regents of the University of California). Used with permission.

summarizes the evidence for both learning and acquisition of grammar. It acknowledges that students must first learn the rule or rules. This is an important acknowledgment. Students cannot be expected to simply infer all of the rules for the language. Although we believe that, given time, most students would be able to infer many of the rules, we don't have unlimited amounts of time for students to do so. We can accelerate their learning by providing them with information about the rules.

It is also important to note that the graphic clearly indicates that learning the rule or rules is not enough. Students must also *use* the rule to produce authentic speech or writing. As they do so, students notice the errors they make and revise their production such that it fits with the rules. Vickers and Ene (2006) documented the importance of English language learners noticing and correcting their own grammatical errors. In their research on standard English learners, Rickford (1999) and Rickford and Rickford (1995) note that teaching the rules and helping students monitor their use of the rules in specific situations is helpful as they improve their skills using standard academic English.

As the graphic also notes, students use their output as a source of input. When students use their own voice or writing for feedback and monitoring, they gradually generalize the rule to new situations and learn the structure. Over time, with significant practice and feedback, students acquire the new grammatical feature. This extends learning—

Table 4.2. Grammar Learning Process

Step in Learning Process	Definition	Example
Learns Rule	The learner memorizes a rule.	The learner learns to put an –*s* on the end of verbs with singular subjects.
Uses Rule	The learner thinks about the rule and applies it.	The learner starts to say, "John go to school."
Produces Output	The learner produces language using the learned rule.	The learner says instead, "John goes to school."
Uses Output as Input	The learner's own output serves as input.	The learner processes his or her own output and considers the correctness of the output (e.g., Yes, that sentence was correct).
Acquires New Grammatical Feature	Input triggers acquisition of structure.	The learner acquires the third person –*s* morpheme.

knowing the rule—to acquisition—*using* the rule with automaticity in authentic and unique situations.

It is important to recognize that teaching grammar is most effective when it takes place within the context of reading and writing. A focus on sentence structure, usage, and even paragraph organization must be combined with an understanding of the characteristics of text. Traditional methods of teaching writing have taken a bottom-up approach—beginning with basic rules of grammar from which students learn to write sentences, from which they learn to write paragraphs, from which they learn to write essays. As we look at student writing—sentences, paragraphs, and essays—we find at least three sources of errors: knowledge of rules, knowledge of the writing process, and understanding of the characteristics of different types of text (Robinson & Tucker, 2005). Clearly, we must teach the rules that govern the organization of sentences. However, this addresses only one of the sources of student errors. We believe that a top-down approach to teaching writing and grammar, where making meaning is the primary goal, allows students to place these rules in the context of meaningful communication for a specific purpose. The approach to teaching grammar that we describe in this chapter integrates phonetics, phonology, semantics, and pragmatics with morphology and syntax. It teaches effective use of academic language at the word level, the sentence level, and the discourse level.

Contrastive Rhetoric

Contrastive rhetoric (Kaplan, 1966) is an additive approach to teaching writing and an effective way to teach grammar within authentic contexts. It is based on the theory that languages (and vernaculars) differ from each other in significant ways—semantics, morphology, grammar, rhetoric, and phonology. If we define *rhetoric* as the ability to use language effectively, and *contrastive* as the study of similarities and differences between two languages (contrastive, n.d.), we can define *contrastive rhetoric* as an approach to teaching writing that teaches students to use language effectively by examining the similarities and differences between standard academic English and other languages or vernaculars.

Instruction based on contrastive rhetoric uses both reading and writing to teach students to construct sentences, paragraphs, and essays that effectively accomplish the intended purpose. It is a highly contextualized method of instruction that integrates language and content as students deconstruct and analyze text, learning to use the language, organization, rhetorical devices, and conventions appropriate to a variety of academic genres.

In this chapter we discuss the importance of using student writing to teach grammar. Their writing alone, however, does not afford the opportunity to teach all the structures and conventions they need. They simply do not use a wide enough variety of grammatical structures. Teaching students to read rhetorically allows us to model and provide explicit instruction on structures they need in order to comprehend and use language in academic situations. Teaching students to read rhetorically means using text to focus students' attention on both content (what the text is saying) and process (how the author presents the content) (Bean, Chappell, & Gillam, 2005). Through this process we can focus on grammar as well as comprehension, teaching standard academic English structures and syntax along with word choice and organization. In addition to providing exemplars of grammatical structures, it is also a way to ensure that students use higher-order thinking skills as they learn grammar. In all too many ESL/ESOL classes, we do not expect students at early levels of language proficiency to think critically. An abundance of tasks that require repetition of grammar patterns, yes/no responses, or simple retelling can result in an ever-widening achievement gap as native-English-speaking students engage in tasks where they hone their skills in analysis and synthesis and apply their learning in a variety of ways.

In the gradual release of responsibility model of instruction, reading rhetorically is the modeling phase, which is particularly valuable for ELL students who may need more models than native-English-speakers. Since not all students will need to focus on the same grammatical structures, small group instruction is an excellent way to provide the additional modeling that many ELLs need.

Teaching students about language through a contrastive rhetoric approach can take many forms. Students can read a piece of text and then rewrite it for another purpose. Groups of students might read a newspaper report of an event and rewrite it as an editorial, a poem, a narrative with plot, setting, conflict and climax, or even as a part of a history textbook with supporting graphics. Standard English learners might rewrite it in the vernacular they use with their peers, or they might write a text in their vernacular and then rewrite it in standard academic English. A rubric for scoring can detail expectations for their writing. Through the rubric, teachers might require students to use literary devices such as symbolism or foreshadowing, or expect them to include specific language structures such as prepositional phrases or past tense. Another way for students to examine differences in language is to rewrite a popular song as an expository essay. In order to accomplish these tasks, they must deconstruct the content and the language of the text. They also must analyze the language and the strategies that are characteristic of the particular genre they have been assigned (or selected) to write. As a class they can then analyze the differences in the vocabulary, language structures, organization, and rhetorical devices used to address the same event in different genres. They can use graphic organizers to compare and contrast the language and vocabulary of the original text with the language and vocabulary of the new versions.

Language Transfer

Many errors that we see in student writing are direct translations of structures from their primary language. Although there is virtually no way for teachers to know these patterns in the many languages of our students, attention to the patterns of errors can often reveal those that may be a result of language transfer. You can then use contrastive analysis to teach the standard English structure. Table 4.3 contains some examples of grammatical structures found in other languages and vernaculars.

Instructional Strategies for Focusing on Grammar

Now let's consider some instructional strategies and classroom routines that are useful in students' acquisition of grammar. Based on our experiences, we believe that the vast majority of grammar instruction should be conducted with small groups or individual students. We know that grammar learning is not linear and that different students have mastered different structures. This mastery is often related to their heritage or home language, the extent of their understanding of universal grammar rules, the transferability of specific rules from the first to the second language, and grammar instruction in previous years of schooling. We are concerned that teachers waste significant amounts of time with scripted grammar programs in that there are always students who have mastered the specific rules, students who are moving from learning to acquisition, and students for whom the grammatical structure is yet unknown. After all, not everyone needs to begin every school year with locating nouns and verbs in sentences. In this chapter, we focus on three instructional strategies that can be useful for students' grammar learning.

Table 4.3. Examples of Transfer from Primary Language Structures

Aspect of Grammar	Language Transfer	Language	Example
Articles	No indefinite articles	Chinese Hmong Korean Vietnamese	He goes to one class on Wednesdays.
Nouns	No plural marker after a number	African American vernacular Chinese Haitian Creole (plural form often omitted) Hmong Korean Vietnamese	There are three new student. Five cent.
Pronouns	No distinction between subject and object pronouns	Chinese Haitian Creole Hmong Spanish Vietnamese	I gave the book to she.
Reflexive Pronouns	Regularized	African American vernacular	My, myself Your, yourself His, hisself Their, theirself
Subject-Verb Agreement	Verb agreement is regularized	African American vernacular Hawaiian-American vernacular Chinese Haitian Creole Hmong Korean (verbs are inflected for age, status) Vietnamese	I was, you was, he was I walk, you walk, he walk
Verbs	Omit the verb *to be* with adjectives and prepositional phrases.	Chinese Haitian Creole Hmong Korean Vietnamese	I hungry. You at home.
	No gerund form or no distinction between gerunds and infinitives	Chinese Haitian Creole Hmong Korean Spanish Vietnamese	She kept to talk.

Source: From *Language Transfer Issues for English Learners* © The Hampton-Brown Company, Inc. Used by permission of The Hampton-Brown Company, Inc. All rights reserved.

Each of the three strategies on which we focus in this chapter allows the English teacher to determine instructional "next steps" based on student writing. We know that students' oral language production is often superior to their written work, so we focus on student writing as a source of information for grammar instruction. Of course, student speaking could also be used to guide instructional interventions. These strategies can be used with the whole class, small groups, or individual students, depending on the performance of particular students and their needs.

Generative Sentences

One approach to grammar instruction involves students constructing sentences from words that are given to them. Fearn and Farnan call this practice a "given word sentence" (2001, p. 87). We have expanded on this practice and note the generative nature of this strategy that carries the writer from the word to the sentence and then to the paragraph level. This strategy allows students to expand their sentences and to be able to use the language and mechanics that are necessary in order to convey information. Essentially, the teacher identifies a letter or word and the place in a sentence where the word will be used. Students then write sentences with the given components.

For example, in their study of a gradual release of responsibility for writing instruction, Fisher and Frey (2003) asked students to write the letter *v* on their paper. The next instruction was to write a word with the letter *v* in the third position. They then recorded a list of these words on the dry erase board. Students were able to see the variation of words that share this characteristic—*love, have, give, dove, advice,* and so on. Following this, students were asked to use their word in a sentence. A sample of the sentences included the following:

- I love my family, especily James.
- The dove is a sign of peace.
- You best get some advice on that hairdo.

On this particular day that the class focused on the letter *v* in the third position, the teacher created a homework assignment from this generative sentence activity. Students were asked to use the sentence they had written as a topic sentence for a paragraph. The paragraphs were due the following day. Students understood that a paragraph could contain three, five, eight, or whatever number of sentences necessary to convey the idea they wanted to share. Consistent with the gradual release model, students had created the topic sentence in class and were well on their way to completing a paragraph for homework. The successful completion rate of this type of homework was much higher than independent writing assignments in which students had to complete the entire paper at home.

Generative sentences can also be used to focus whole class discussions on the craft of writing. Rather than use daily oral language activities to focus on correcting errors, teachers can use samples of students' writing (with names removed). These are then placed on the overhead projector and used to illustrate writing mechanics and craft. For example, in the Fisher and Frey (2003) study, the teacher shared the following sentence written by one of the students: "The car hit the wheelchair guy." Students were asked to talk with a partner about word choice and the impact of the sentence. Each pair was provided with a thesaurus and dictionary. As a whole class, students began talking about the sentence and the event they had witnessed the day before. Slowly they generated new ideas for the sentence and changed it to read: "The distracted driver noticed too late that the wheelchair had entered the intersection. The result was a direct hit."

Early in Abdurashid's language learning, his teachers used generative sentences to expand his understanding of language. For example, during one class session the teacher wanted to focus on adjectives. She asked students to complete the following sentences:

- *Spectacular* in the fourth position of a sentence more than ten words long.
- *Grumpy* in the fifth position of a sentence fewer than nine words long.
- *Inconsiderate* in the sixth position in a sentence of any length.
- *Struggling* in the second position of a sentence more than seven words long.

One of the sentences Abdurashid wrote was "I were in the grumpy mood on Tuesday." His teacher noticed the errors in this sentence as well as the things he did correctly. During her small group instruction, she asked him about his choice of article (*the*). As he reread the sentence, he self-corrected the error (*a*). She then turned her attention to his choice of *were* and asked him about it. He said, "Tuesday is past, so were is right, right?" They talked for a few minutes about singular and plural versions and the impact that changing the pronoun would have (*we were, I was, she was, he was, they were*, etc.).

In a generative sentence session, the teacher provides students with a word or phrase as well as a placement requirement for the sentence. In addition to the word placement, which requires students to control the grammar surrounding the word, teachers can place limits on the length of the sentence to help students develop their sentence fluency. Word limiter activities are helpful for students learning English as they encourage self-editing and a focus on precision in writing (L. Davis, 1998). Sentence fluency—using sentences of varying lengths—is also important for English language learners, as it is one trait of good writing (Culham, 2003).

Generative sentence sessions allow the teacher to assess both content knowledge and understanding of grammar and vocabulary. In this way, the teacher can provide instruction that is responsive to the needs individuals or groups have in terms of their writing.

Sentence Combining

Another excellent approach to grammar instruction also focuses at the sentence level. Teaching students to combine sentences is a powerful way to assess and develop grammar knowledge. For example, Saddler and Graham (2005) compared traditional grammar instruction with sentence-combining instruction and found significantly better results for sentence combining. Connors (2000) noted that sentence combining is a powerful instructional tool, but it declined in use as a result of the "growing wave of anti-formalism, anti-behaviorism, and anti-empiricism" evident in English education after the 1980s (p. 96). W. Smith (1981) noted that sentence combining provides students with an opportunity for discovery, and thus they find it more interesting and engaging. Smith also notes that sentence combining "allows us to show (not tell) students how their [*sic*] rules work in real language" (p. 79). Smith cautions us about the use of sentence combining and notes that students may incorrectly think that combined sentences are better, that complexity is important above all else, or that combined sentences maintain the same meaning and focus as uncombined sentences. The key, notes Smith and others (e.g., Keen, 2004; Saddler, 2005; Shafer, Swindle, & Joseph, 2003), is to use sentence-combining exercises to notice the types of grammar errors students make and then teach them how to address those errors. In other words, sentence combining is not an outcome in and of itself but rather a process for identifying needs and developing instructional interventions.

There are a number of ways to combine sentences, including use of the following:

- **Punctuation**. Students learn that some punctuation marks end sentences (period, question mark, exclamation mark) and others allow for sentences to be combined. It is important that students know that the comma is not powerful enough to combine sentences. Simply using a comma to combine two sentences will likely result in a run-on sentence or comma splice. The punctuation marks that do allow for sentence combining are the dash (—), colon (:), and semi-colon (;).
- **Compound sentences**. Another way to combine sentences is through the use of compound sentences. Students learn to use specific words to create compound sentences when the ideas are equal to one another. The words that connect ideas, or clauses, in this way are called coordinating conjunctions, and the most common ones are *and, or, but, so, because*.
- **Subordination**. Combining sentences to make one sentence more important than the other is done through subordination. These complex sentences have a main clause or independent clause and one or more subordinate clauses or dependent clauses. The words *when, although, if* (called subordinating conjunctions) or the words *who, what, that* (called relative pronouns) are commonly used in subordination.
- **Reduction**. A way to combine sentences even further is to change one of the sentences to a phrase. This reduction results in a few added words to the main sentence such that the new sentence contains important details from the sentence being reduced to a phrase.
- **Apposition**. An appositive is like a parenthetical statement surrounded by commas, not by parentheses. This final way for teaching students sentence combining results in students understanding how to take a word or phrase and place it in a parallel position to a noun in the sentence.

These five main ways to combine sentences require sophisticated knowledge of grammar and not simply memorized grammar rules. As students engage in sentence combining, the teacher notices the types of errors being made and provides supplemental instruction for students. Let's consider the following classroom example of a teacher using sentence combining to focus instruction on grammar.

Raquel was contacted by her English teacher just before her senior year of high school to deliver a short speech to welcome the faculty back from summer break. Her first draft was adequate but not fluent, with choppy sentences and few transitions. Her English teacher met with her to discuss how her sentences could be combined to enhance the flow of the message, a task Raquel initially found a bit overwhelming. The teacher printed the twenty-two sentences on individual strips of paper and arranged them on the desk in front of Raquel. Using scissors and tape, the two of them cut sentences apart in order to recombine them. For example, Raquel's draft contained these sentences:

> My family immigrated from Mexico. They live in a small town and they do not have a phone. I don't get to talk to them.

They discussed punctuation and reduction as methods for combining, as well as the need to clarify the meaning, and soon they arrived at the following:

> My family immigrated from Mexico—my parents still live in a small town there and I don't get to talk with them because they don't have a phone.

They moved on to three more choppy sentences:

> Families have disagreements sometimes. But we care about each other. We offer to help people all the time.

Using apposition and dependent clauses, they transformed these sentences into one strong statement:

> As a family, we might have disagreements or hard times, but we care about each other and we offer to help people in our family all the time.

In short order, Raquel had tightened her speech to fifteen sentences and improved the fluency and flow of the piece. Her speech on the first day of school for teachers follows:

> Thank you for inviting me to speak to you. I would have never thought I would be doing this. I am Raquel Ramirez-Gomez and Tuesday I become a senior at Hoover. I would like to thank you all for being part of my life. My family immigrated from Mexico—my parents still live there in a small town and I don't get to talk with them because they don't have a phone. You have become my family. As a family, we might have disagreements or hard times, but we care about each other and we offer to help people in our family all the time. You have been that family to me. The people in the health center, the counselors, principals, everyone has been amazing and has become my family. Like a family, you believe in me and all of the other students like me. It means a lot. I hope to go to college when I graduate. No matter where I go, you will all go with me. As I learned from South Park, "Family isn't always about whose blood you have. It's about who you care about."

Sentence Syntax Surgery

Performing syntax surgery consists of writing student-constructed sentences onto sentence strips, cutting apart the sentence in "problematic" places, and rearranging the words into a correct English sequence. Students then practice reading the sentence in the correct English word order and follow by practicing more sentences with the same grammatical pattern. Syntax surgery, therefore, is a strategy designed to make English syntax, grammar, and structure more visible to English language learners. Sentence syntax surgery is also useful as a visual tool for standard English learners who often experience difficulty with code switching between their home language patterns and the standard English used in school (Wheeler & Swords, 2006).

Several years into her secondary schooling experience, Arian was still making minor errors in grammar as she spoke and wrote. Her teacher used sentence syntax surgery to help her understand the specific places where she made errors. It is important to note that highlighting errors too early in the language development process—such as with students at the Entering or Beginning levels—is likely to result in delayed growth as students may become so focused on their errors that they refuse to speak or write (Campbell, 1996; Krashen, 1985).

During one class period, Arian wrote, "The character he was dangerous." Her teacher wrote this sentence on a sentence strip and cut out the word "he" as Arian and she talked about the correct formation of the sentence. On another day, she wrote a sentence much like she talks, "It is blue?" Although this might work orally, used with facial expressions and a raised tone at the end of the sentence, it does not work in writing. Using sentence syntax surgery, they changed the word order to "Is it blue?"

Leadership in English

Work on grammar is mainly the role of the English teacher in middle and high school. However, with support from English teachers, content area teachers can facilitate students' understanding and use of correct grammar structures. As Adger, Snow, and Christian (2002) noted, there are many teachers who are not sufficiently comfortable with their own grammar knowledge to teach grammar to students. Lily Wong Filmore and Catherine Snow (2000) suggest that teachers need to understand how language works if they are to help students reach academic proficiency. Table 4.4 summarizes areas of knowledge that these researchers believe are critical for teachers to understand.

English teachers can provide resources and support for their colleagues to facilitate grammar learning schoolwide. Robin Scarcella (2003) identified ten major areas of focus for grammar instruction for English language learners: sentences, subject-verb agreement, verb tense, verb phrases, plurals, auxiliaries, articles, word forms, fixed expressions/idioms, and word choice. Definitions and examples of each of these can be found in Table 4.5.

Although we do not position grammar instruction per se as a schoolwide instructional strategy, content area colleagues may be interested in learning the ways in which they can support the use of accurate grammar usage in their classrooms.

1. *Use corrections to speech production judiciously.* As stated earlier, corrections to grammar and pronunciation, while well meaning, can have the opposite effect on English language learners in the early stages. Allow speakers to complete their thoughts without rushing or interrupting them. Restate and rephrase their answers so that they can hear a more sophisticated production of the language ("So you're noticing . . ."). This ensures that other students in the class, as well as the English language learner, are hearing an accurate model, without putting the student on the spot.

2. *Provide feedback on written work that is instructive, not evaluative.* Many colleagues in content areas have not learned about instructive written feedback and therefore fall back on their own memories of secondary school assignments. Even sophisticated writers are stumped about what to do next when the abbreviation *awk* (awkward) is scrawled in the margin. Seemingly random application of underlined words and phrases is also decidedly unhelpful. Share a short list of editing marks with colleagues so that they can utilize a more instructive set of feedback marks that provide the students with information about what to do next. Although not all editing marks are directly related to grammar (they include capitalization, spelling, and such), they do allow a means for correcting errors in writing. A style guide of common editing marks appears in Figure 4.3.

3. *Don't tell them that their use of good writing techniques "doesn't count."* We've heard teachers too often tell students before a writing assignment that "——— doesn't count" (spelling, grammar, punctuation, and so on).

Table 4.4. What Teachers Need to Know about Language

What Teachers Need to Know	Instructional Implications
1. What are the basic units of language? ■ Phonemes, morphemes, words, phrases, sentences, paragraphs, extended discourse	■ Understanding the variety of structures used in different languages can help teachers see the logic behind student errors of and thereby help correct them ■ Help students learn and refine English phrasing and syntax
2. What's regular and what isn't? How do forms relate? ■ There are regular patterns in word formation	■ Teach principles of word formation to help students acquire new vocabulary (e.g., the *d* changes to *s* in *persuade/persuasive* ■ Teach students to parse new words ■ Use native language structures to help students learn—*idad = ity, curiosidad = curiosity*
3. How is the lexicon acquired and structured? ■ In context, related to topics students are interested in ■ Depth of knowledge about words is as important as breadth of knowledge.	■ Provide exposure to new vocabulary in related groups ■ Teach related word forms
4. Are vernacular dialects different from bad English and if so, how? ■ Perception of standard dialects as more prestigious than vernacular dialects is a matter of social convention, not of utility	■ Recognize the effect of language on adults' perception of students ■ Provide instruction in the English required for school while respecting the language of the home
5. What is academic English? ■ Cognitively demanding language in decontextualized settings requiring wide knowledge of words, phrases, grammar, and pragmatics	■ Focus on language across content areas ■ Students need to be able to use language to summarize, analyze, evaluate, interpret, extract information, use correct grammar, compose coherent and cohesive text ■ Provide multiple opportunities for text interpretation, identification of essential contextual clues, key academic vocabulary terms that help manage content and derive meaning
6. Why has English acquisition not been more successful? ■ English language learners may not have received the explicit instruction needed to master academic English	■ Programs that build native language proficiency promote acquisition of English ■ Provide opportunities to interact with fluent English speakers

continued on next page

Table 4.4. continued

■ Students with strong first language backgrounds may acquire English rapidly	■ Provide an English-rich environment ■ Teach structures explicitly ■ Provide corrective feedback
7. Why is English spelling so complicated? ■ English has borrowed words from many languages, retaining original spelling of morphological units	■ Student errors reflect lack of exposure to written forms, lack of explicit instruction, or transfer from home language ■ Teach principles of word formation
8. Why do students have trouble with structuring narrative and expository writing? ■ Students may bring culturally based text structures that conflict with those expected of them at school.	■ Provide explicit instruction in English text structures ■ Provide many models of standard English text structures
9. How should one judge the quality and correctness of a piece of writing? ■ Teachers need to understand the structure of English	■ Discuss structural features of English ■ Explicitly teach structures needed to understand and produce good writing ■ Provide informed feedback to help students become effective writers
10. What makes a sentence or a text easy or difficult to understand? ■ Simplified text may make content uninteresting, incoherent, and unnatural, and provide less information ■ Oversimplified text does not model academic English ■ Complex sentences provide necessary cohesion of ideas and details and make texts more readable	■ Amplify information rather than simplify language ■ Provide support for students to access well-written text with grade-level appropriate language

Source: *What Teachers Need to Know about Language,* by L. Wong Fillmore & C. Snow, 2000 (Washington, DC: Office of Educational Research and Improvement, U.S. Department of Education).

Table 4.5. Ten Grammar Structures English Language Learners Need to Know

Rule of Grammar	Example	Incorrect Use
1. Sentence Structure All sentences have one subject and one main verb. A main verb is not a part of an infinitive that begins with *to.*	My English *instructor* in high school *was* the key person who taught me.	My English *instructor* in high school *key person* to teach me.
2. Subject-Verb Agreement Subjects agree with verbs in number. Indefinite pronouns such as *everyone* are generally followed by singular verbs.	*Everyone understands* me.	*Everyone understand* me.
3. Verb Tense Use the present tense to refer to events that happen now and to indicate general truth. Use the past tense to refer to events that took place in the past. Generally use the present perfect with words such as *already, yet, since* + a number of years.	My instructor *explained* how important books *are* for students.	My instructor *explain* to me that how important the books *was* for the student.
4. Verb Phrases Certain verbs are followed by *to* + the base form of a verb while others are followed by a verb that ends in *–ing.*	My instructor persuaded me *to read* many books.	My instructor persuaded me *read* many book.
5. Plurals A plural count noun *(table, book, pencil)* ends in an –s.	My instructor persuaded me to read many *books.*	My instructor persuaded me read many *book.*
6. Auxiliaries Negative sentences are formed by using *do* + *not* + the base form of the verb.	Please *do not make* me lose face.	Please *do not makes* me lose face.
7. Articles Definite articles generally precede specific nouns that are easily identifiable because they are modified by adjectives.	I don't speak *the Vietnamese* language.	I don't speak *Vietnam* language.
8. Word Forms The correct parts of speech should be used. Nouns should be used as nouns. Verbs should be used as verbs, etc.	I have *confidence* in English.	I have *confident* in English.
9. Fixed Expressions and Idioms Idioms and fixed expressions, such as *to lose face,* cannot be changed in any way.	Please do no make me *lose face.*	Please do not make me *lose the face.*
10. Word Choice Formal words should be used in formal settings. Informal words should be used in informal settings.	Dear *Professor Scarcella:*	Dear *Robbin,*

Source: Adapted from *Accelerating Academic English: A Focus on the English Learner,* by R. Scarcella, 2003 (Oakland, CA: Regents of the University of California). Used with permission.

Mark	Meaning	Example
caps ≡	Capitalize this letter	English language learner
lc /	Make this letter lowercase	English language Learner
ℊ	Delete	English language learner ~~students~~
^	Replace	learners English language ~~students~~
^	Insert	language English learners
tr	Transpose word order	English learners language
¶ ∟	New paragraph	English language learners
⊙	Add a period	English language learners attend this school
^ ,	Add a comma	English language learners use their back-ground knowledge, experiences and interests as they read.
^ : ^	Add a colon	English language learners speak many languages Spanish, Tagalog, Hmong, etc.
; ^	Add a semicolon	Adolescent English language learners are unique they possess many life experiences.
" / "	Quotation marks	Some English language learners can be described as members of Generation 1.5.

Figure 4.3. Editors' marks. In some cases, you'll need two marks, a reinforcing mark in the margin (top) and an in-text mark (bottom).

Just as the content counts, so does the way in which the ideas are conveyed. Instead, remind them to write "as well as you can" in all situations.

Conclusion

> My attitude toward punctuation is that it ought to be as conventional as possible. The game of golf would lose a good deal if croquet mallets and billiard cues were allowed on the putting green. You ought to be able to show that you can do it a good deal better than anyone else with the regular tools before you have a license to bring in your own improvements. (Ernest Hemingway)

As Hemingway suggests, and we concur, students need to understand the basic rules of grammar. Of course, in our creative writing, personal journals, poems, raps, and the like, we all take poetic license to break grammar rules. The difference is that proficient users of the language know that they are breaking the rules and play with the language accordingly.

These grammar conventions can be taught in ways that are dynamic and motivating to students. These include using generative sentences, sentence combining, and sentence surgery to focus on aspects of grammar instruction needed by an individual learner, so that the rules become more meaningful to the student. Adolescent English language learners possess unique profiles of grammatical knowledge that are influenced by their home language, schooling experiences, and idiosyncratic communication styles. While Arian may ask, "It is blue?" and still have her meaning understood in a conversation, meaningful grammar instruction gives us an opportunity to expand her ability to communicate to a wider audience.

5 Focus on Fluency: More Than the Need for Speed

Great is our admiration of the orator who speaks with fluency and discretion.
Marcus Tullius Cicero

As Cicero noted, fluency in speaking (as well as in reading, we would argue) is part of what we expect from an educated person. Being able to read, write, and speak fluently is widely recognized as a sign of intelligence and sophistication. In other words, fluency matters in the lives of individuals who want to engage in civic debate, participate in social events, and join in the world of work. Cicero also notes that discretion, knowing what to share and when, is an important part of public life. As we saw in Chapter 1 (Table 1.1), discretion, or pragmatics, is key to the sociolinguistic, discourse, and strategic components of proficiency. In this chapter, we focus on the fluency that Cicero so admired, a skill that reflects the phonological, lexical, and grammatical components of language proficiency.

What Is Fluency?

Fluency is often defined as reading in which words are recognized automatically. While that is an important component of fluency, the concept involves much more. We know that once students attain automatic word recognition, reading becomes faster, smoother, and more expressive. This is all part of fluency. The rate at which you read, speak, or write is important. But so is prosody—the speech elements such as intonation, pitch, tempo rate, stress, loudness, and rhythm—that speakers and readers use. Of course, writers not only have to write fluently but also use conventions to guide their readers' fluency. Writers have at their disposal a number of tools such as rhythm, alliteration, rhyme, and dialogue to guide their readers.

Our definition of fluency is a bit more encompassing and involves being facile in speech, reading, and writing. This contrasts with some common definitions of fluency as a measure of speed. Let's consider each of the three major components of fluency: oral, reading, and writing.

Oral Fluency. Oral fluency typically relates to the ways in which people speak. It involves both speed and prosody. For English language learners, it also involves pronunciation. For all students, but especially standard English learners, it involves an understanding of language registers. As we discussed in Chapter 2, there are a number of students who violate accepted norms for language registers, using slang and casual registers when the context, environment, or milieu requires a more formal tone. As a profession, we do not have norms for oral speaking fluency that are not connected with reading text passages. We do expect students to be able to speak at rates that are comfortable for the listener and to use prosody appropriately. However, Burgess (1999), Morley (1991), De la Colina, Parker, Hasbrouck, and Lara-Alecio (2001) remind us that speaking rates and oral fluency vary based on native language, bilingual status, cultural expectations about such elements as pauses, and comfort in the situation.

Reading Fluency. Researchers have learned significantly more about reading fluency than speaking fluency. Rasinski and his colleagues have conducted extensive research on reading fluency for students in elementary (Rasinski, 2000), middle (Rasinski & Padak, 2005), and high school (Rasinski et al., 2005). These studies clearly demonstrate the importance of fluency in literacy development. They suggest that reading fluency, both silent reading and oral reading fluency, are important instructional considerations (Rasinski, 2004). As a profession, we have identified norms for reading fluency (e.g., Hasbrouck & Tindal, 1992). For example, by eighth grade, students at the 90th percentile read about 199 words per minute while students at the 25th percentile read about 124 words per minute. Although these tables and norms are important, there are some simple indicators that suggest that a student's reading fluency requires attention or intervention, including when a student reads:

- Haltingly
- Word by word
- With little or no expression

Writing Fluency. Another area of focus in the context of fluency is writing. Although it receives even less attention than oral fluency, our experience suggests that writing fluency is an important instructional consideration (Fisher & Frey, 2003). We know, for example, that writing prompts impact writing fluency (Hudson, Lane, & Mercer, 2005). We also know that we can assess students' writing fluency and improve their performance in this area (Leal, 2005). An instructional focus on writing fluency can improve writing performance and achievement (Fisher, Frey, et al., 2004; Kasper-Ferguson & Moxley, 2002). As with speaking fluency, we do not have norms for writing fluency. The fourth graders in the Kasper-Ferguson and Moxley (2002) study averaged 25 words written per minute, with one student consistently writing 60 words per minute. In our ninth-grade classroom, students averaged 33 words per minute.

Of course, our goal is not just to get students to write fast, any more than our goal is to get students to simply read more quickly. In our writing fluency work, we must provide students with strategies for producing increasingly complex compositions. In part, writing fluency develops from practice with timed writings. It also happens as we provide students with writing frames that they can use in their writing. As students incorporate these frames into their writing habits, they become quicker writers as well as better writers who can enter the academic conversations that writers have with their readers.

Why Is Fluency Important for English Language Learners?

The sounds used in a given language differ from those in other languages. Babies are born with the ability to hear all sounds in all languages. By the age of six months, however, due to lack of exposure to other sounds, they can now hear only those sounds of their own language, and their brain must be retrained in order to fully hear the sounds of another language (Zadina, 2005). The degree of overlap between two languages has a significant impact on the literacy development—both in terms of speed and production. Spanish, for example, has a fairly high degree of overlap with English whereas Vietnamese does not. Importantly, there are specific sounds used in English that are absent in other languages. This is one of the reasons that Dutro and Moran (2003) note that students need to learn English and not just *in* English. Students will not develop fluency—oral, reading, or writing—from simply being exposed to the language (Palumbo & Willcutt, 2006).

Fluency, as we have noted, is part of what makes us sound educated. As such, fluency impacts our ability to get a good job, participate in the economy, and engage with other human beings. Fluency is also directly related to comprehension. If you can't read fast enough, with good prosody, comprehension is impeded. As August and Shanahan (2006) note, fluency is one of the critical language skills and is too often missing for English language learners.

Reynolds (2005) examined essays from 189 English language learners and 546 native English speakers for their linguistic fluency, which he defines as "the use of linguistic structures appropriate to rhetorical and social purposes" (p. 19). His analysis and findings suggest that the differences in linguistic fluency can be attributed to the ESL students' limitations in grammatical competency and a lack of practice in writing. Lack of linguistic fluency is one of the primary reasons that students remain protracted at intermediate levels of English proficiency and do not become skilled users of the language. It's not a coincidence that we call students who reach the highest levels of English proficiency "fluent English learners."

Instructional Strategies for Focusing on Fluency

> Talking is one of the fine arts—the noblest, the most important, the most difficult—and its fluent harmonies may be spoiled by the intrusion of a single harsh note. (Oliver Wendell Holmes)

We are not sure what Holmes meant by a "harsh note," but we agree that talking is one of the fine arts. We begin our discussion of instructional strategies on just that—oral fluency. We then explore instructional strategies for improving reading fluency before turning our attention to writing fluency.

Oral: Private Rehearsal and Practice

While effective communication can happen with a limited vocabulary and simplified sentences, proper pronunciation is critical. Benrabah (1997) underscores the importance of verbal skills in suggesting "no matter how good a non-native learner is in grammar and lexis, this competence is likely to lead nowhere unless she/he acquires a 'threshold level of pronunciation' below which communication is simply non-existent" (p. 157).

Rhythm and intonation are often the most difficult aspects of pronunciation for English language learners to master (Chela-Flores, 1994). Both rhythm and intonation contribute to a speaker's overall intelligibility, which can be defined as "the extent to which a speaker's message is actually understood by a listener" (Munro & Derwing, 1999, p. 286) or "the way someone says something" (Levis, 1999, p. 38).

Mary Jewell, a high school English and ESL teacher, focused on pronunciation as part of the homework she provided her students. She thought that tape recorders might help her students focus on the sounds used in the language. In a study by Yule and Macdonald (1995), students who listened to tapes of native speakers pronouncing key vocabulary and then practiced and recorded themselves using the same words, showed more pronunciation improvement than students not provided this experience.

Before assigning the homework, she met with a group of students and explained the procedure they would use each week. Ms. Jewell demonstrated how to play and record tapes using handheld tape recorders. She prepared cassette tape recordings of herself reading a short passage from a book. The texts she selected for each student matched their independent reading levels. Students in Ms. Jewell's class engage in independent reading with books of their choice every day, so texts were selected from the classroom library. These types of "authentic texts provide a realistic model of language use . . . to raise learners' awareness of language features" (Basturkmen, 2002, p. 27).

Ms. Jewell also gave the students a photocopy of the passage and a blank tape for them to record themselves reading the passage. Each time they received a new passage and tape, students were asked to listen to their teacher read the passage and then to record their own reading of the passage. Over several days, they listened to their teacher's recording and rerecorded their own voice. They were asked not to record over their previous attempts, but rather to keep adding to the tape. After several days of practice, students returned the tapes, both the one with their teacher's voice and the one that they recorded. This type of private practice allowed students to focus on their pronunciation without being called out in class. Ms. Jewell used the recordings to monitor her students' progress and to plan individualized instruction based on what she heard.

Over the course of this intervention, students in Ms. Jewell's class improved their pronunciation as well as their overall fluency. One of the students, Jose, wrote in his journal: "I like this project because it really helps me speak English better. I listen more now because I want to speak well, like the people from the United States."

Oral: Public Speaking

On a recent talk show, people were asked to describe their greatest fear. Many said that it was public speaking. Since that isn't one of our fears, we decided to ask our students about this. Sure enough, they would just about do anything to avoid public speaking. As we listened to these students share their concerns about public speaking we were reminded of a quote from E. M. Forster (1879–1970), " I didn't know what I thought about it until I heard what I said about it." Sharing thinking publicly, either through speaking or writing, is one of the ways that we clarify our own thinking.

One of the reasons students tell us that they do not like public speaking is because they feel judged. To a certain extent, they're right. People judge other people based on their ideas and presentation of those ideas. If you doubt this, think about the judgments you make about public speakers within the first ten seconds of listening, whether the contact is via the phone, television, lecture hall, or classroom.

For adolescent English language learners, there is an added dimension to this fear of judgment. Teenagers, in general, are highly affected by what their peers think of them, and are loathe to make mistakes of any kind in front of others. Students who are not yet proficient in English, by definition, will make mistakes—in pronunciation, in grammar, in word choice. They are often reluctant to speak out and thus miss out on the very practice that would help them improve.

Another reason students tell us that they do not like public speaking is that they are uncertain what to do. They do not feel prepared and do not know what "quality work" looks and sounds like. James Chesebro, past president of the National Communication Association, suggested that "lack of oral communication skills is one our most critical national problems." Students need instruction in public speaking. They need to realize that the ideas they are sharing orally must be crafted so that the contents as well as the mechanics are appropriate to the audience and situation. They need time to practice many types of public speaking (e.g., conversations, debates, interviews, and speeches). When doing so students need to be taught the following:

- The many contexts in which they speak (e.g., home, community, classroom, workplace) require adjustments in information presented as well as in style of presentation (e.g., speech, conversation, reading).
- The context determines the audience.
- Both the familiarity the audience has with the speaker and the topic influence the speaker's selection of tone, vocabulary, grammar, and amount of information (detail) conveyed.

As teachers, we must prepare our students for public speaking. We know that they will not all become great orators or consultants who travel the globe collecting huge speaking fees. We do believe that every one of our graduates should be able to share his or her thinking with a group of people and that they should not break out in a cold sweat when asked to do so. We also know that oral language development will facilitate print literacy. As August and Shanahan (2006) note, there is a correlation between oral fluency and print (reading and writing) fluency.

1. *Only experts can be good public speakers.* Good speakers are knowledgeable about their subject, but they don't have to know everything.
2. *Speeches are serious business.* Audiences appreciate a warm smile and a friendly look. Don't be silly, but don't be wooden, either.
3. *Don't make eye contact, because it will make you nervous.* Making eye contact personalizes your speech.
4. *Write your whole speech, or even better, memorize it.* You'll sound too robotic—use a natural speaking style and have a short list to remind you of your main points.
5. *Stand still.* Audiences like some movement from speakers. Stand in different areas, use your hands, and turn your head.
6. *You're more nervous than other people about public speaking.* Everyone gets "butterflies"—remember that your audience wants you to succeed.
7. *The worst thing that can happen is making a mistake.* If you make a mistake, smile and regroup. If it's a noticeable mistake, acknowledge it and move on. In most cases, the audience never notices the mistakes you think are so obvious.

Figure 5.1. Seven myths about public speaking.

As part of our work on oral fluency, we must address the stress associated with public speaking. As noted in Figure 5.1, there are a number of myths related to public speaking. Fortunately, most of these are the product of fear and are easily addressed. It is critical that students understand this and that we directly confront the fear factor on a regular basis. Providing ample opportunities to practice speaking with a partner and in small groups is one sure-fire way to build confidence and reduce anxiety.

As we confront the fear related to public speaking, we need to provide students with instruction in public speaking. They need to be able to speak on impromptu topics and to share their thinking in more formal settings. In middle and high school English classrooms, most teachers focus on two types of speeches: persuasive and informational.

Persuasive Speeches. "It is impossible to escape persuasive speaking, and persuasion has consequences. Change can occur when persuasion takes place. Persuasion is the process that occurs when a communicator (sender) influences the values, beliefs, attitudes, or behaviors of another person (receiver). . . . To fully understand persuasion, we need to understand influence and motivation." (Hybels & Weaver, 2000, p. 458)

Informational Speeches. "Informative speeches generally concentrate on explaining—telling how something works, what something means, or how to do something. A speaker who gives an informative speech usually tries to give his or her audience information without taking sides." (Hybels & Weaver, 2000, p. 293)

As one of her rotations during her English language arts instruction, Ms. Javier has students select impromptu speech topics. As they arrive at this particular center, students in the group (usually numbering four or five) select a slip of paper from a large container. On the slip is written a topic—either a word or phrase. Through her whole class modeling, Ms. Javier has taught her students about impromptu speeches. During the beginning of the term, they are required to state their opinion or main idea and to provide two supporting statements. They are also required to summarize their opinion or main idea as a closing. Over time, she will work with her students on an opening hook to their impromptu speeches, adding details, acknowledging alternative views, and challenging the audience. However, Ms. Javier knows that most of her students have little experience with public speaking, and she wants to provide them with some basic skills in sharing their thinking orally.

On a particular day, Abdurashid was at the public speaking center. He selected the topic "marriage" from the container. He had twenty minutes to work on his topic, get ideas from the other four students in the group, and rehearse.

All of the students in Ms. Javier's class work in collaborative centers while she meets with specific groups of students to provide direct instruction. Every twenty minutes or so they change stations. As part of the transition between stations, the students at the public speaking center share their speeches with the class. Abdurashid said:

> Couples from different social classes may face several difficulties in their marriage. Due to the fact that our backgrounds, culture, and values shape our personalities, it is often difficult for couples from different socioeconomic classes to bind with common interest, which is essential for marriage. These differences may include personal preferences, expectations, and educational goals. Couples from different social backgrounds can fall in love and get married, but they will face some complications. In some cases interclass marriage is beneficial because it helps broaden one's knowledge. However, one has to know that there are countless dissimilarity, conflict of ideas, and very hard compromises to be made in order to make it work.

As he speaks, members of his group provided feedback using the rubric in Figure 5.2. Abdurashid used this feedback to revise his speech and discussed the revisions during conference time with his teacher.

Name: ____________________

When__________ speaks in a group, he/she:

	Score	Comments
Sticks to the topic.		
Builds support for the subject.		
Speaks clearly.		
Takes turns and waits to talk.		
Talks so others can hear.		
Speaks smoothly.		
Uses courteous language.		
Presents in an organized and interesting way.		
Supports the topical thesis.		
Answers questions effectively.		
Is comfortable speaking publicly.		
Maintains listeners' interest.		

A = always, S = sometimes, N = never

Figure 5.2. Speaking checklist. *Source*: Adapted from "An Integrated Approach to the Teaching and Assessment of Language Arts," by D. Lapp, D. Fisher, J. Flood, & A. Cabello, 2001. From Hurley, Sandra Rollins & Josefina Vilamil Tinajero *Literacy Assessment of Second Language Learners*, 1/e. Published by Allyn and Bacon, Boston, MA. Copyright © 2000 by Pearson Education. Reprinted by permission of the publisher.

Abdurashid received very positive comments from his group about the contents of his speech and his ability to hold the listeners' interest. However, they all noted that his voice was a bit hard to hear and that he doesn't make a lot of eye contact with the audience. Two of the group members also noted that he should try to speak more smoothly and that he should practice his words (vocabulary and pronunciation) a bit more before standing up to speak.

During his conversation with his teacher, Abdurashid said, "See, they like what I say. I just need to make some confidence. I will look at them next time but not lose my place." Ms. Javier commended his logical flow, his thinking, and the development of his public speaking and suggested ways that professional speakers interact with their audience. She offered, "You know, really good speakers like to make eye contact with specific people and then scan the room. You know what that means, to scan the room? You look around the room without really looking at any one person. But high-paid speakers usually do this between sentences, especially between sentences that have a lot of impact. That way they don't lose their place. Some speakers even make a little mark to remind them to look up. They can use that mark to find their place again. Well done. Didn't it feel great to share your ideas?"

Reading: Repeated Readings

Research suggests that repeated reading is an effective way to improve students' reading fluency (Dowhower, 1994). When reading the same piece of text over and over, the number of word recognition errors decreases, reading speed increases, and oral reading expression improves (Samuels, 2002). Repeated reading also improves word recognition, comprehension, and recall of information (Herman, 1985; Rasinski, 1990). Unfortunately, teachers have a hard time getting students to engage in repeated readings. Many students, especially adolescents, do not see the value in reading something that they have already read before.

To encourage repeated reading, teachers can use a variety of instructional routines and procedures. Repeated reading can be used in small group instruction, one-on-one with a particular student, following a whole class shared reading, or in partners. Regardless of the structure, the goal is to encourage students to reread a familiar piece of text and, in doing so, read it faster and with more prosody.

One of the ways that middle and high school English teachers use repeated reading involves partner reading. For example, during their collaborative learning time, Arian and her partner were reading a selection from *Woman Hollering Creek* (Cisneros, 1991) called "Salvador, Late or Early." Their teacher, Mr. James, had modeled fluent reading a number of times with the class. On this particular day, students were working with partners to reread and discuss texts. Arian used the rubric in Figure 5.3 as a discussion starter with her partner.

During one of their exchanges, Arian noted that her partner had increased the speed of the reading as well as the number of words pronounced well. As part of the feedback she provided, Arian said to her

I noticed that my partner:	Second Reading	Third Reading
Read faster	Yes No	Yes No
Used more vocal qualities (tone, pitch, volume)	Yes No	Yes No
Read more smoothly	Yes No	Yes No
Read with expression	Yes No	Yes No
Used punctuation as a guide for reading	Yes No	Yes No
Remembered more words and read them automatically	Yes No	Yes No

Figure 5.3. Rubric for repeated readings.

partner, "You read faster, I could tell. But what about the voice—it was the same. Can you go slow in some places and fast sometimes? That would make it interesting, you know, like when he runs that would be faster."

Reading: Readers Theater

As noted earlier, motivation can play a factor in getting students to engage in repeated readings. Readers theater is a performance-based fluency-building strategy that fosters comprehension as well as prosody through dramatic reading of scripts (Busching, 1981). Unlike traditional theater, performers do not memorize lines, wear costumes, or use props and staging. Instead, they convey the meaning of the piece through voice alone, much like a radio play. Each character's lines are chorally read so that an individual student is not solely responsible for the accuracy and expression needed for the part.

Readers theater scripts are widely available on websites devoted to the practice, but the best can often be found within the texts students are reading in class. Poetry, of course, is a natural source for a readers theater treatment and carries the added bonus of providing students with the power of the spoken word as a poetic device. Plays come with scripting intact, and even passages of dialogue from novels lend themselves to readers theater. Often overlooked are the dramatic speeches of history—Sojourner Truth's "Ain't I a Woman?" Lincoln's Gettysburg Address, Lou Gehrig's "Farewell to Baseball." These texts first lived as spoken word and come alive again through the collaborative performance of a readers theater.

Rehearsal is the key to readers theater. Students read and discuss the script, divide parts, practice, and provide feedback to one another. Therefore, readers theater typically extends over several class periods to allow for peer collaboration. Many English teachers use a five-day schedule similar to the one described by Martinez, Roser, and Strecker (1998–1999):

> **Day 1**: Teacher introduces script and discusses content, including vocabulary. Assessment and performance expectations are established.
>
> **Day 2**: Teacher echo-reads script with students to model fluency and prosody; students meet to discuss script and choose roles.
>
> **Day 3**: Students continue to rehearse sections of script, focusing on accuracy and fluency; teacher assists.
>
> **Day 4**: Rehearsal of entire script; students finalize decisions about performance.
>
> **Day 5**: Readers theater performance and assessment.

Of course, all this rehearsal means that students *must* engage in repeated readings in order to refine their performance. Since there is no memorization (in fact, it is discouraged), their eyes are passing over text again and again, an act that appears to contribute to their reading fluency (Opitz & Rasinski, 1998). McCauley and McCauley (1992) found that choral reading was particularly effective for English language learners because of its inherently social nature, the low risk to individuals, and the high motivation of peer collaboration.

Reading: Neurological Impress Method

Neurological Impress Method (NIM) is possibly one of the easiest and most cost-effective methods of developing children's fluency. Heckelman (1966) designed NIM based on methods that had been used with students with stuttering problems. He first used this approach to address the needs of a ninth-grade student identified with significant reading difficulty. He noted that this student read "in a stumbling, halting fashion that could hardly be identified as reading" (Heckelman, 1969, p. 278). After twelve hours of NIM instruction spread over time, this ninth-grade student improved her reading proficiency by three grade levels. Other researchers have also documented positive changes in fluency after using NIM (Flood, Lapp, & Fisher, 2005; Hollingsworth, 1970).

NIM procedures suggest that the teacher and student hold the text together with the student sitting slightly in front of the teacher. As the teacher moves her or his finger under each word and speaks directly into the dominant ear of the student, they read the text together in a fluent manner pausing only where punctuation dictates (Arnold, 1972). As part of the NIM experience, Heckelman believed that teachers should positively reinforce their students. He believed that "this close physical, one-to-one relationship of the teacher and the student contributes to a psychological affect component" (Heckelman, 1969, p. 415). According to Flood, Lapp, and Fisher (2005), steps for the NIM include the following:

- The teacher selects a text within the student's reading level.
- The teacher sits at the student's side so that he or she can speak into the student's ear.
- The student's finger rests on top of teacher's finger as they read.
- The teacher moves her finger under each word as it is spoken.
- The teacher reads aloud slightly faster than the student reads aloud and models good fluency (chunking phrases and stopping where punctuation dictates).
- The teacher gives the "lead" to the student as the student becomes comfortable with the text. (p. 149)

The only complication with NIM is that it requires individualized instruction. Although this is not possible for every student in the class, when there are English language learners who have difficulty with fluency, this is the strategy of choice. For example, when Raquel was in her second year of school in the United States, we used NIM to rapidly increase her reading fluency. On one afternoon, Raquel read a newspaper article with her after-school tutor. The tutor used NIM to improve Raquel's fluency. Of course, they had a short conversation about the article when they finished reading it. Raquel recalls reading individually with her tutor and says, "I like it. We read together two times per week. I felt a little pressure, a bit, you know, to get better than Dan. It help me read faster and understand my reading."

Writing: Power Writing

Writing fluency is less frequently addressed in classrooms yet plays the same critical role as speaking and reading. The ability to receive and express information smoothly allows the communicator to focus more on content, rather than mechanics. Students are often assessed using timed writing prompts, yet they have little experience outside of the testing event to increase their writing fluency. The result is well known to teachers. After delivering some encouragement to a student who has failed to start after several minutes, the student responds, "I'm thinking!" These writers may not possess the writing fluency needed to get down to the business of composing. This further impacts their writing negatively because they may have never felt the flow of composition that more fluent writers count on to carry them to the end of the piece.

Power Writing is a method for building writing fluency through brief, timed writing events (Fearn & Farnan, 2001). The purpose is to get students to put ideas down on paper rapidly. We use a simple daily routine of three one-minute rounds, and students keep a notebook or journal containing all their writing. We remind students to "write as much as you can, as well as you can" (p. 196). We then post a word or phrase on the board and ask students to use it somewhere in their writing. We set the timer, and students write until it rings a minute later. When time is up, they reread what they have written, circling any errors they notice, and then count and record the number of words in the margin. This routine is repeated two more times, until there are three one-minute writing samples in their journals. They record the highest number of words written (often it is the third sample) on a sheet of graph paper kept in their notebook (see Figure 5.4 for an example). Over time, students see their progress as they become more adept at putting ideas down on paper.

There are a number of variables that can be manipulated to suit the needs of the students. For instance, the time can be extended to two minutes or five. The content focus may be grammar:

- Homophones (*carrot*, *carat*, and *caret*)
- Singular and plural possessives
- Irregular verbs

At other times, the focus may be on content learning:

- Literary devices (*mood*, *tone*, and *theme*)
- Vocabulary (*narcissistic*, *draconian*, and *stoic*)
- Character traits of Sophie in *Eyes, Breath, Memory* by Edwidge Danticat (*secretive*, *introspective*, *resilient*)

Daily Power Writing serves as an excellent formative assessment for fluency, content knowledge, and grammar. Teachers can gain insight into the kinds of errors that are occurring in the class, as well as noting what a student is noticing (and not noticing). There is less concern about

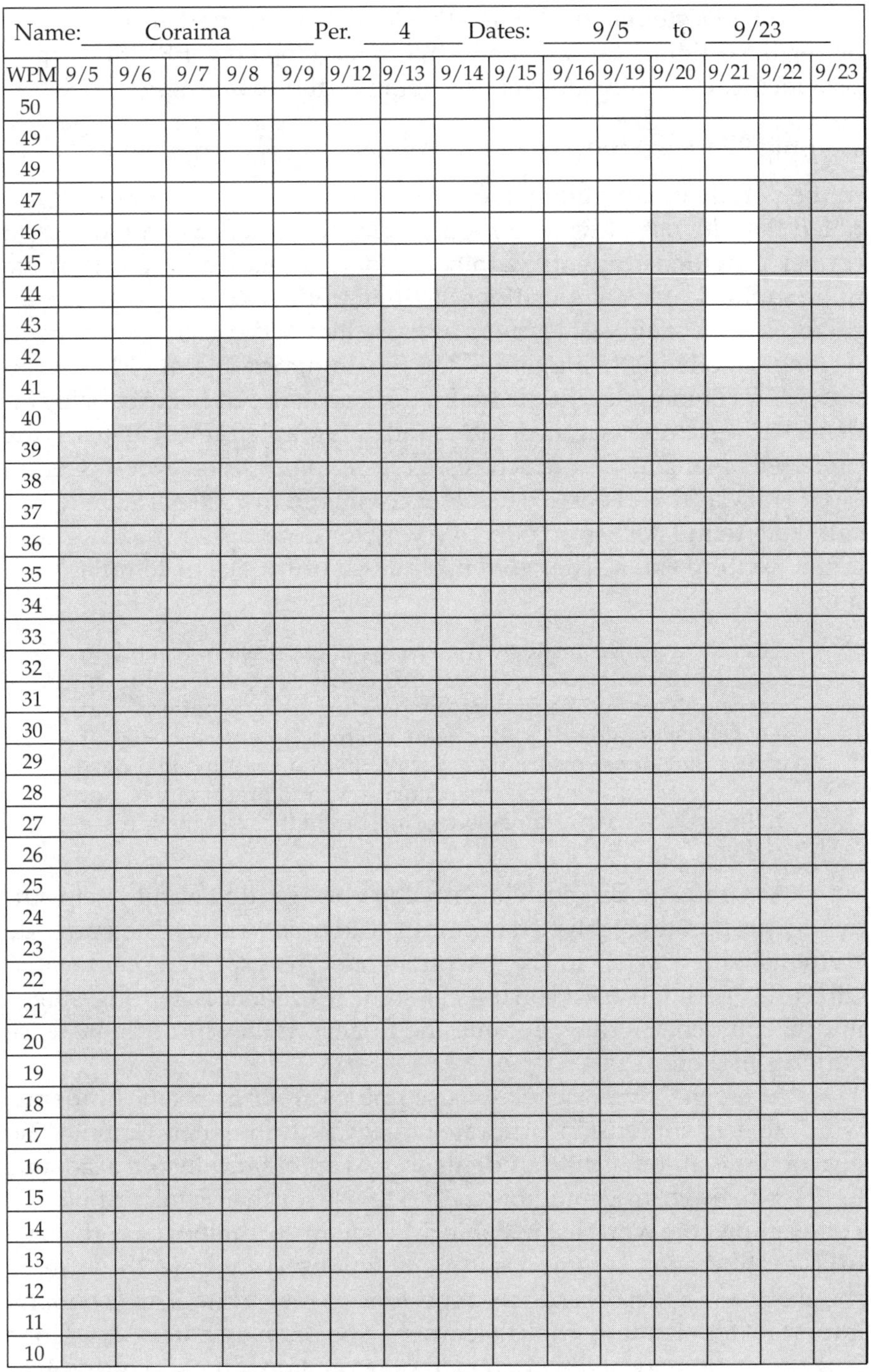

Name: Coraima Per. 4 Dates: 9/5 to 9/23

WPM	9/5	9/6	9/7	9/8	9/9	9/12	9/13	9/14	9/15	9/16	9/19	9/20	9/21	9/22	9/23
50															
49															
49															
47															
46															
45															
44															
43															
42															
41															
40															
39															
38															
37															
36															
35															
34															
33															
32															
31															
30															
29															
28															
27															
26															
25															
24															
23															
22															
21															
20															
19															
18															
17															
16															
15															
14															
13															
12															
11															
10															

Figure 5.4. Power Writing graph on graph paper.

an error that a student has circled than one that goes undetected by him or her. In addition, the daily data collected on the Power Writing graph provides quick visual information about individual progress.

Writing: Sentence and Paragraph Frames

In their study of struggling adolescent writers, Fisher and Frey (2003) noted that the use of writing models such as sentence and paragraph frames provided students with scaffolds that enabled them to write more sophisticated compositions. Writing frames are particularly helpful for English language learners because they serve as models of good writing—modeling being one of the most important scaffolds we can provide for students as they learn English. Sentence frames can help students learn grammatical structures, and paragraph frames can teach the preferred organizational structures. College composition experts Gerald Graff and Cathy Birkenstein (2006) recommend the use of frames (they call them templates) as an effective way for developing students' academic writing skills. They defend the use of frames or templates by noting,

> After all, even the most creative forms of expression depend on established patterns and structures. Most songwriters, for instance, rely on a time-honored verse-chorus-verse pattern, and few people would call Shakespeare uncreative because he didn't invent the sonnet or dramatic forms that he used to such dazzling effect. . . . Ultimately, then, creativity and originality lie not in the avoidance of established forms, but in the imaginative use of them. (pp. 10–11)

As Graff and Birkenstein correctly note, writing frames help students incorporate established norms of academic writing. They provide students with practice in the discourse patterns expected of educated citizens. In addition, based on our classroom experiences, writing frames improve students' writing volume and fluency as they incorporate these patterns into their craft.

At the most basic level, we use frames around specific academic words to help students incorporate target words into their writing. The goal of this is automaticity: students should automatically use academic terms in their writing and not need to revise for their choice of words. For example, the word list in Table 5.1 contains a number of verbs useful for introducing summaries and quotations. Over time, these verbs should become part of students' repertoire as they write. This is equally important for standard English learners who often do not use academic language automatically and, in fact, may not know these words. Over

Table 5.1. Verbs for Introducing Summaries and Quotations

Function	Verbs	
Making a Claim	■ argue ■ asset ■ believe ■ claim ■ emphasize ■ insist	■ observe ■ remind us ■ report ■ suggest
Expressing Agreement	■ acknowledge ■ admire ■ agree ■ celebrate the fact that ■ corroborate ■ do not deny	■ endorse ■ extol ■ praise ■ reaffirm ■ support ■ verify
Questioning or Disagreeing	■ complain ■ complicate ■ contend ■ contradict ■ deny ■ deplore the tendency to ■ disavow	■ question ■ refute ■ reject ■ renounce ■ repudiate
Making Recommendations	■ advocate ■ call for ■ demand ■ encourage ■ exhort	■ implore ■ plead ■ recommend ■ urge ■ warn

Source: Adapted from *"They Say/I Say": The Moves That Matter in Academic Writing* by Gerald Graff & Cathy Birkenstein. Copyright © 2006 by W. W. Norton & Company, Inc. Used by permission of W. W. Norton & Company, Inc.

time and with instruction in the use of these terms, Abdurashid regularly incorporated these verbs into his writing. Consider the following excerpt from an essay he wrote in favor of the community service requirement:

> In sum, community service plays an important role in the process of learning. It's not enough to encourage students to participate in some sort of voluntary work before graduation, we should insist on it. I believe that the more students engage in helping others, the better the nation will be. Community service reminds us all about the reality of the world and what is going on around us. When I arrived in the U.S., it was an American citizen who

> volunteered to show me the Pacific Ocean for the first time in my life. He said that he was urged to volunteer for his community and this helped him in becoming a good citizen in a new country. I strongly recommend that community service remain a graduation requirement.

Dutro (2005) noted that writing frames are especially effective with English language learners. For example, she suggests the use of the following sentence frame to help students write a compare/contrast essay: "_______ and _______ share several characteristics, including ______." Arian used this frame in comparing a character from the novel *The Turning Hour* (Mickle, 2001) and her own suicide attempt when she wrote, "Bergin and I share several characteristics, including the fact that she tried to kill herself, she was upset about her life, and that she knew she was loved."

Raquel used a paragraph frame developed by Graff and Birkenstein (2006) in her essay on immigration. The opening paragraph, which is based on a writing frame, reads:

> When it comes to the topic of immigration, most of us will readily agree that the US is a nation of immigrants. Where this agreement usually ends, however, is on the question of the rights of immigrants. Whereas some are convinced that immigrants should be given all of the rights a US citizen has when they arrive, others maintain that these rights must be earned and that not everyone can have these rights.

Writing frames are typically based on a careful analysis of writers' craft or the moves writers use. When English language learners are taught to read with the added lens of identifying these moves that writers use to inform, persuade, or entertain their readers, they begin to incorporate the moves into their own writing (Nichols, 1980). In addition, teachers can create any number of sentence and paragraph frames for their students to use. With repeated practice with writing frames, both at the sentence and paragraph level, students become increasingly proficient in their writing, and this writing becomes increasingly academic (Jones & Thomas, 2006).

Leadership in English

The formal concept of fluency in reading, writing, and oral language is not widely known outside of the field of English yet is universally recognizable to content area teachers through their observations of student learning. When talking with colleagues in other departments, listen for descriptors that suggest students have difficulties with fluency:

- Reticence of English language learners to speak in front of the class
- Slow and choppy reading styles that interfere with comprehension
- Low output and precision of written language
- Difficulty in starting or sustaining writing

Some fluency-building strategies discussed in this chapter are useful in content area classes, especially explicit public speaking instruction to accompany oral presentation projects in science, readers theater study of speeches in history, and Power Writing in all content areas to rehearse the use of academic language and concepts before writing.

English teachers can also take a leadership role in student activities to build fluency. Consider sponsoring a student activities club that emphasizes oral fluency, such as a chapter of the National Forensics League (www.nflonline.org) or Toastmasters Youth Leadership Program (www.toastmasters.org). Students interested in the creative writing of poetry and performance can be organized into a Poetry Slam club. The Youth Speaks organization was established a decade ago to foster spoken word performance and has chapters in thirty-six cities (www.youthspeaks.com).

Conclusion

> I am just now beginning to discover the difficulty of expressing one's ideas on paper. As long as it consists solely of description, it is pretty easy; but where reasoning comes into play, to make a proper connection, a clearness and moderate fluency, is to me, as I have said, a difficulty of which I had no idea. (Charles R. Darwin)

Oral, reading, and writing fluency are essential for development of language proficiency. Adolescent English language learners are doubly challenged because they are learning content at the same time as they are developing their language skills. Therefore, it is essential to use fluency instruction in service of content learning. Oral fluency strategies such as private and public rehearsal and oral presentations are connected to purposeful instruction in extemporaneous and rhetorical styles of engagement. Readers theater and repeated readings build reading fluency and become meaningful when used in conjunction with the content text.

These performances carry the additional benefit of reinforcing comprehension by drawing attention to the relationship between the written form and the spoken word. This can be especially significant when used with evocative poetry, dialogue, and speeches. Finally, writing fluency can be increased through daily Power Writing practice. Done correctly, these are not mindless drills but rather are used to promote the use of academic language in writing. Power Writing serves as a motivational tool for students, who chart their own progress as they become more fluent at getting their ideas down on paper. As Abdurashid noted, "They like what I say." Fluency instruction ensures that readers, writers, and speakers make themselves understood to others.

6 Focus on Comprehension: "The Cooperation of Many Forces"

A very complex procedure, involving the weighing of each of many elements in a sentence, their organization in the proper relations to one another, the selection of certain connotations and the rejection of others, and the cooperation of many forces to produce the final response.

Edward Thorndike

Comprehension has been described as the "gold standard" of learning. After all, the skills and strategies taught in the English classroom are for naught if understanding is sacrificed. However, a challenge of comprehension is that it is, ultimately, internal to the learner. In this chapter, we discuss the concept of comprehension, its importance to English language learners, and instructional approaches for fostering comprehension.

What Is Comprehension?

There are a number of different ways to view comprehension. Perhaps the most common is Benjamin Bloom's taxonomy of learning behaviors in the cognitive domain (Bloom, Englehart, Furst, Hill, & Krathwohl, 1956). In this model, comprehension is a learner's ability to make meaning of the ideas, concepts, and skills taught. It is beyond the knowledge level, which emphasizes recall alone. Learners who comprehend are able to explain, interpret, predict, and discuss.

This skills-driven approach to comprehension has given way to other lenses through which comprehension is viewed, including attempts to define it by factors such as word meaning and idea relationships (Simons, 1971). Most educators today describe reading comprehension using the language of strategies identified in studies of effective readers. These studies revealed that effective readers are oriented toward specific strategies and actions, particularly monitoring their comprehension, and utilizing techniques for regaining and maintaining meaning, such as activating background knowledge, questioning, clarifying, making predictions, and evaluating the information (Paris,

Wasik, & Turner, 1991). This consolidation and use of these comprehension strategies, such as Thorndike's "cooperation of many forces," lies at the heart of instruction that results in meaningful comprehension.

Effective Comprehension Instruction

It is essential to be clear on what comprehension is in order to provide effective instruction on using comprehension strategies. Over the past two decades, a number of instructional approaches have proven successful with a wide range of readers, including English language learners. The National Reading Panel (2000) summarized research evidence for the following eight reading comprehension strategies:

1. *Comprehension monitoring* in which readers learn how to be aware or conscious of their understanding during reading and learn procedures to deal with problems in understanding as they arise.
2. *Cooperative learning* in which readers work together to learn strategies in the context of reading.
3. *Graphic and semantic organizers* that allow readers to represent graphically (write or draw) the meanings and relationships of the ideas that underlie the words in the text.
4. *Story structure* from which readers learn to ask and answer who, what, where, when, and why questions about the plot and, in some cases, map out the time line, characters, and events in stories.
5. *Question answering* in which readers answer questions posed by the teacher and are given feedback on the correctness.
6. *Question generation* in which readers asks themselves why, when, where, why, what will happen, how, and who questions.
7. *Summarization* in which readers attempt to identify and write the main or most important ideas that integrate or unite the other ideas or meanings of the text into a coherent whole.
8. *Multiple strategy instruction* in which readers use several of the procedures in interaction with the teacher over the text. Multiple-strategy teaching is effective when the procedures are used flexibly and appropriately by readers or the teacher in naturalistic contexts. (pp. 4–6)

That last finding is particularly crucial. Too often, we have seen a reductive approach to comprehension instruction, with discrete strategies taught in isolation from one another. For example, we have been in classrooms where summarizing is taught out of context, cut off from the other comprehension strategies with which it interfaces, such as question generation and text structure. Therefore, summarizing becomes a two-week unit taught early in the semester, disconnected from previous learning and never revisited once the unit is over. Researchers have continually stressed the importance of integrated instruction (e.g., Beck, McKeown, Hamilton, & Kucan, 1997; Raphael, 1984, 1986; Keene & Zimmerman, 1997), yet the lure of discrete comprehension units has proven too strong for some teachers. We have included a glossary of comprehension strategies in Figure 6.1 in an effort to show how strategies are linked to one another.

Why Should Comprehension Be a Priority for English Language Learners?

In a study of English-proficient Iranian students reading two encyclopedia entries written in English on Iranian and Japanese culture and belief systems, students comprehended texts written from their own cultural experiences more deeply than those passages that were written from an unfamiliar perspective (Malik, 1990). Interestingly, their comprehension was not impacted at the sentence level, where they did quite well. Rather, it was their comparative difficulty at integrating and evaluating new information that posed a problem. In other words, even these more fluent English learners found it challenging to understand text at the meta-level.

Simply stated, background knowledge is critical to comprehension. A problem with building background knowledge, however, is that some teachers use the typical approach of telling, rather than teaching. For English language learners, this is problematic, and the result is a jumble of disjointed facts that are not integrated into a schema, and therefore not easily retrieved when needed. (Most of us recall a time in our schooling when we tried to memorize a list of facts rather than really learn the subject because the facts seemed meaningless, unrelated to our lives, or not connected to our understanding of the "real world.")

Building Background with English Language Learners

> Knowledge is of two kinds: we know a subject ourselves, or we know where we can find information upon it. (Samuel Johnson)

We have discussed methods for building background in previous chapters, including using read-alouds, shared reading, and vocabulary development. We agree with the observation that "what students take to the text is as important as what they find in it" (WestEd, 2002b, p. 1). Adolescent English language learners present a unique challenge to the

Reading Comprehension Glossary of Terms

Cause and effect—text structure used to explain the reasons and results of an event or phenomenon. Signal words for cause include *because, when, if, cause,* and *reason.* Words like *then, so, which, effect,* and *result* signal an effect (e.g., Fisher & Frey, 2004).

Compare and contrast—text structure used to explain how two people, events, or phenomenon are alike and different. Some comparison signal words are *same, at the same time, like,* and *still.* Contrast signal words include *some, others, different, however, rather, yet, but* and *or.*

Connecting—linking information in the text to personal experiences, prior knowledge, or other texts. This is commonly taught using three categories (Keene & Zimmerman, 1997):

- Text to self—personal connections
- Text to text—connections to other books, films, etc.
- Text to world—connections to events in the past or present

Determining importance—a comprehension strategy used by readers to differentiate between essential information and interesting (but less important) details.

Evaluating—the reader makes judgments about the information being read, including its credibility, usefulness to the reader's purpose, and quality.

Inferencing—the ability to "read between the lines" to extract information not directly stated in the text. Inferencing is linked to a student's knowledge of vocabulary, content, context, recognition of clues in the text, and experiences.

Monitoring and clarifying—an ongoing process used by the reader to ensure that what is being read is also being understood. When the reader recognizes that something is unclear, he or she uses a variety of clarifying strategies, including rereading, asking questions, and seeking information from another source.

Predicting—the reader uses his or her understanding of language, content, and context to anticipate what will be read next. Prediction occurs continually during reading, but is most commonly taught as a pre-reading strategy.

Problem/solution—text structure used to explain a challenge and the measures taken to address the challenge. Signal words for a problem include *trouble, challenge, puzzle, difficulty, problem, question,* or *doubt.* Authors use signal words for a solution like *answer, discovery, improve, solution, overcome, resolve, response,* or *reply.*

Question-Answer Relationships (QAR) (Raphael, 1984, 1986)—Question-answer relationships were developed to help readers understand where information can be located. There are four types of questions in two categories.

(1) *In the Text*—these answers are "book" questions because they are drawn directly from the text. These are sometimes referred to as text-explicit questions:

- Right There—the answer is located in a single sentence in the text

continued on next page

Figure 6.1. Glossary of reading terms. *Source*: Frey, Nancy; Fisher, Douglas B., *Language Arts Workshop: Purposeful Reading & Writing Instruction,* 1st,©2006. Electronically reproduced by permission of Pearson Education, Inc., Upper Saddle River, New Jersey.

Figure 6.1. continued

- Think and Search—the answer is in the text but is spread across several sentences or paragraphs

(2) *In Your Head*—these answers are "brain" questions because the reader must generate some or all of the answer. These are sometimes called text implicit questions:

- Author and You—the reader combines information from the text with other experiences and prior knowledge to answer the question
- On Your Own—the answer is not in the text and is based on your experiences and prior knowledge

Questioning—a strategy used by readers to question the text and themselves. These self-generated questions keep the reader interested and are used to seek information. Specific types of questioning includes QAR, QtA, and ReQuest.

Questioning the Author (QtA) (Beck et al., 1997)—an instructional activity that invites readers to formulate questions for the author of the text. The intent of this strategy is to foster critical literacy by personalizing the reading experience as they consider where the information in the textbook came from and what the author's intent, voice, and perspectives might be.

Synthesizing—the reader combines new information with background knowledge to create original ideas.

Summarizing—the ability to condense a longer piece of text into a shorter statement. Summarizing occurs throughout a reading, not just at the end.

Temporal sequence—a text structure used to describe a series of events using a chronology. Signal words and phrases include *first, second, last, finally, next, then, since, soon, previously, before, after, meanwhile, at the same time,* and *at last.* Days of the week, dates, and times are also used to show a temporal sequence.

Visualizing—a comprehension strategy used by the reader to create mental images of what is being read.

English teacher because their background knowledge is far less predictable than that of a younger student. Their collective life experiences and previous schooling result in individualized profiles; no two students are alike. This also means that the teacher cannot assume that the background knowledge needed to understand a text or unit is in place. Thus, building background requires a two-pronged approach: activating prior knowledge to build schemas and providing advance organizers for new learning (Hill & Flynn, 2006).

Leveled Questions. The heart of activating prior knowledge lies in questioning, in inviting students to consider what they know about a topic. This act allows students to begin constructing and expanding schema of what will be learned (Anderson & Pearson, 1984). Leveled questioning is particularly effective for English language learners at the early stages of development (Herrell, 2000). Students respond to questions that are phrased to be comprehensible and consistent with their current language level. For example, a student at the earliest phase of development would nod or use gestures to respond, while a student at the intermediate level would be able to respond with longer sentences. Use of leveled questions is critical to find out what students already know, especially for those who are less proficient users of the language. We caution teachers to plan their questions carefully to ensure that all students, including those with little English, are encouraged to think critically about the content. It is easy to mistake silence for lack of knowledge that students actually have or, alternatively, for understanding that they do not have. With leveled questions, teachers have a technique for eliciting responses. A table of leveled questions can be found in Table 6.1.

Advance Organizers. The second element in building background knowledge is providing advance organizers (verbal, written, or visual) to organize the new information that will be learned in a lesson or a unit. An advance organizer can be thought of as an overview of the unit, complete with essential details. This is different from an anticipatory set in a lesson, which is designed to gain attention and build interest. Hill and Flynn (2006) advise that "advance organizers should focus on what is important instead of what is unusual" (p. 48). An effective advance organizer may be verbal but should include pictures or realia so that students are not forced to rely on listening comprehension alone. Visual displays of information, such as graphic organizers, are also useful in alerting English language learners to the connections between new concepts (Chamot & O'Malley, 1996). Finally, advance organizers can be used in written form, for students to read and discuss at the beginning of a lesson. In all cases, students should refer back to the advance organizer so that they can monitor their own learning. This promotes metacognitive awareness, the final piece of comprehension instruction.

Metacognitive Awareness and English Language Learners

> There are many that I know and I know it. Always now slowly I understand it. (Gertrude Stein)

Comprehension instruction is ultimately wasted if the learner is unaware of how to apply the tools to support his or her own reading. After all, the purpose is to develop a student's ability to read and under-

Table 6.1. Leveled Questions

Stage of Language Development	Expected Student Response	Example of Leveled Question
Entering	■ Graphic representation ■ High-frequency words ■ Memorized phrases	■ Match ■ Identify ■ WH questions with visual support ■ Select the one that....
Emerging	■ Phrases ■ Short sentences ■ Uses some language of content area	■ Describe ■ List ■ What happened next?
Developing	■ Expanded sentences with errors in grammar	■ How are ____ and ____ alike or different? ■ What do you think will happen next?
Expanding	■ Longer sentences with more linguistic complexity and minimal errors ■ Uses some technical language of content area	■ Summarize ■ How did you . . . ? ■ What would you do . . . ?
Bridging	■ Extended discourse ■ Uses technical language of content area	■ Why did the author . . . ? ■ What might have happened if . . . ? ■ Justify

Source: Adapted from *PreK–12 English Language Proficiency Standards* by TESOL. Copyright 2006 by Teachers of English to Speakers of Other Languages. Reproduced with permission of Teachers of English to Speakers of Other Languages in the format Textbook via Copyright Clearance Center.

stand text without the constant support of the teacher. Therefore, it is important to teach for metacognitive awareness, the ability to recognize one's own learning and to act upon it. English language learners who are in classrooms where metacognition is fostered are found to be more successful in their second language reading (Hosenfeld, 1977). Carrell studied the metacognitive awareness of young adults who were native Spanish speakers and found that the strategies they applied to reading differed depending on whether it was written in their first or second language, and that global metacognitive awareness (activating background knowledge, attending to text structure) was associated with higher reading levels (1989).

Instructionally, metacognitive awareness is promoted through a variety of techniques, including the use of teacher modeling through think-alouds, guided comprehension strategy instruction, and peer conversations about texts. In the section that follows, we explore each of these approaches to improving comprehension with English language learners.

Instructional Strategies for Focusing on Comprehension

In English classrooms across the country, teachers focus on reading comprehension. There is not a state in the union that does not have comprehension as a central tenet of English language arts standards. Understanding that, we focus the remainder of this chapter on specific comprehension strategies with high utility for English language learners, knowing that English teachers are already devoting instructional time to this important idea.

Think-Aloud

As we discussed in Chapter 2, all students need access to teacher modeling as part of their learning experience. This is especially helpful for English language learners as they incorporate thinking, in English, about texts. Think-alouds are a powerful way for teachers to share their comprehension strategies through modeling. Think-alouds can be done during storytelling, read-alouds, or shared reading. The major difference between these approaches is whether or not there is a text (no text is used in storytelling) and whether or not students see the text as the teacher reads. In read-alouds, the students listen as the teacher reads, whereas during shared readings the students follow along with their eyes as the teacher reads.

The history of think-alouds is interesting. Between about 1960 through the 1980s, think-alouds were used as a research tool. Teachers and researchers used think-alouds to understand students' cognitive processes, thinking, problem solving, and comprehension. During this era, the students spoke (thought aloud) while reading so that the teacher or researcher could gain a glimpse of their cognitive processing (Afferbach & Johnston, 1984; Olshavsky, 1977).

Beginning in the 1980s, the use of think-alouds shifted. Teachers and researchers understood that think-alouds could be used to model for students the strategies good readers use to comprehend texts. The goal was to encourage all students to use the strategies that were modeled in their own thinking and reading comprehension (Davey, 1983; Paris, Lipson, & Wixon, 1983).

Today, think-alouds are used as an essential component of the social interactions teachers and students use as they make meaning of texts. In other words, thinking aloud is now viewed less as strategy and more as "an aspect of social interaction, specifically as an aspect of the discourse in social contexts designed to teach reading comprehension" (Kucan & Beck, 1997, p. 272).

Figure 6.2 contains a number of tips helpful in planning think-alouds. Recall that we have already discussed the comprehension strategies that you might use as think-alouds (Figure 6.1). In the example that follows, the teacher links her think-aloud to other classroom interactions, thus creating a social milieu in which reading processes and reading comprehension are facilitated through conversation. As Kucan and Beck (1997) argue,

> When students participate in discourse environments and engage in dialogue or communication, their learning is not confined to knowledge constructed as a product in such a context, but also includes a developing understanding of and ability to use the processes by which such knowledge is constructed. For example, in discussion about text in which students communicate their developing understanding of text ideas and listen as other students do the same, students would be expected to construct not only an understanding of the text content but also an understanding about the process of constructing meaning from text. (p. 290)

In the following lesson (see Figure 6.3), Ms. Johnson, a sixth-grade English language arts teacher, models comprehension strategies through a think-aloud method by analyzing the main character through his actions and the actions of others. She has selected a passage from *Maniac Magee* (Spinelli, 1990). In this passage the title character adds to his growing legend among his peers in a pitching duel with the best Little League baseball player in town, John McNab. Notice how she provides an advance organizer as well.

Ms. Johnson begins the lesson by distributing photocopies of the passage and placing a similar copy on the overhead projector. She reminds her students that they should mark their photocopy of text by underlining or highlighting key points. "We're going to look at how an author, Jerry Spinelli, uses action to tell us about a character. In this passage, we're going to read about the time when Jeffrey batted against the best pitcher in town. After we finish reading, we're going to write down the actions we see and add them to our character chart. Because

Choose a short piece of text.

Think-alouds are most effective when they are focused and well paced. A brief think-aloud delivered using a passage of one to four paragraphs will make more impact because student interest is maintained. As well, it prevents the temptation to model too many strategies.

Let the text tell you what to do.

Don't plan to think aloud using cold text, because your teaching points will be unfocused. Read the text several times and make notes about the comprehension strategies you are using to understand. These will provide you with ideas for the content of your think-aloud. Annotate the text so you will have something to refer to as you read.

Keep your think-alouds authentic.

It can be a little disconcerting to say aloud what's going on in your head. Most teachers adopt a conversational tone that mirrors the informal language people use when they are thinking. An overly academic tone will sound contrived. It's better to say, "Hey—when I read this part about the penguins, right away I saw a penguin in my mind," rather than, "I am metacognitively aware and activated my visualizing strategy to formulate an image of a penguin as I read that paragraph."

Think like a scientist, mathematician, historian, artist, literary critic. . . .

Your shared reading texts are chosen because they have content value. Thinking aloud does not mean that everyone suddenly has to be a reading or English teacher. Make your think-alouds authentic by telling students how you process text through the lens of *your* content expertise. This elevates the think-aloud because you are showing them how your understanding of content text is influenced by what you know about the content.

Tell them what you did.

Using an authentic voice doesn't mean you can't name the strategy. Tell your students what strategy you used to help you comprehend. This allows them to begin to form schemas about reading comprehension. Underline or highlight words or phrases that helped you understand and encourage students to do likewise, if possible.

Resist the urge to "overthink."

The meaning of the passage should not be sacrificed for the sake of the think-aloud. Avoid inserting so many think-alouds into the reading that the intended message is lost. Fewer well-crafted think-alouds will have far more impact than a stream-of-consciousness rap that leaves the students bewildered by what just happened.

Figure 6.2. Tips for effective think-alouds. *Source*: Adapted from Fisher, Douglas B.; Frey, Nancy, *Improving Adolescent Literacy: Content Area Strategies at Work*, 2nd,©2008. Electronically reproduced by permission of Pearson Education, Inc., Upper Saddle River, New Jersey.

Assessed Need *I have noticed that the students in my classroom need to work on:*	Inferring character traits—especially how the author tells about a character through actions
Standards	McREL LA Std. 6.II.6: Makes inferences from or draws conclusions about characters' qualities and actions
Text	Reading from *Maniac Magee* (Spinelli, 1990)
Materials	Excerpt on overhead transparency, chart paper for notes, markers
Purpose	To describe character traits of Jeffrey (Maniac)
	SEQUENCE OF FOCUS LESSON
Model	Parts to emphasize: Read text and stop at designated points—use think-alouds at paragraph beginning: "And then somebody new stepped up to the plate."
Scaffold	Questions to ask: What does the author tell us about Jeffrey? What do John McNab's actions tell us about Jeffrey? What do Maniac's actions tell us about him?
Coach	*Students practice with partners* With your partner, chart the reactions of the children who are watching the pitching duel. What do their actions tell you about what the author wants you to see in Jeffrey? Does this have anything to do with his nickname "Maniac"?
Assess *These are the students who need extra support:*	Check all groups' charts—make sure that Melissa is getting an opportunity to contribute her ideas.
Independent Practice *Students will practice using the strategy during activity time*	Locate an important passage in your group's literature circle and chart how the actions tell you about the character of James, Bud, or Lyddie. What can you infer?

Figure 6.3: Lesson plan for *Maniac Magee.*

the author doesn't come right out and tell you what to think about Jeffrey, we have to use our comprehension strategies to decide what he's trying to tell us." Ms. Johnson gestures to the white board where these steps have been posted in writing.

She places a sheet of paper underneath the transparency so she can block part of the text on the screen while still being able to read it herself and reads the passage to the students while they follow on their copy. She begins reading, adding her think-aloud comments as she goes.

> And then someone new stepped up to the plate. Just a punky, runty little kid, no Red Sox or Green Sox uniform. Kind of straggly. With a book, which he laid down on homeplate. He scratched out a footing in the batter's box, cocked the bat on his shoulder, and stared at McNab.
>
> I'm thinking about what that must have looked liked to everyone else. He's little, he's not on the team, and yet he stares at McNab. That must have seemed pretty gutsy, or brave, considering that McNab had just struck out thirty-five people in a row. I'm going to underline this part so I remember it. I'm *inferring* that Jeffrey is gutsy.

After they have finished the reading, she reviews the events they have marked together and asks them about what the actions of Jeffrey and John tell them about Jeffrey's characteristics. Together with the class, she leads a discussion as they complete a character chart. Now that she is comfortable with their grasp of the concepts so far, she invites them to work in partners to complete the third part of the chart on the reactions of the other children to Jeffrey's feat. While they work as partners, Ms. Johnson checks in with each group to make sure they are making progress. The chart they completed can be found in Figure 6.4.

Guided Comprehension Strategy Instruction

Small group guided instruction is one of the ways that teachers provide comprehension instruction. Meeting with small groups of students to provide direct instruction in areas of need has been identified as one effective way for improving achievement in reading comprehension (Matthews & Kesner, 2003; Tyner & Green, 2005; Urbanski, 2005). It is important to note that these groups are not ability groups, static, or tracked. Instead, groups are formed based on identified student needs. As such, the groups are flexible, and students change groups often. Some students work in a small group with the teacher daily while others work with the teacher once or twice per week. Remember from Chapter 2 that while a small group of students is working with the teacher the rest of the class is working in collaborative groups.

Consistent with the gradual release of responsibility model, the goal of small group guided comprehension strategy instruction is to cultivate independent readers who think about the texts they are reading and understand when and how to use comprehension strategies. The most common comprehension strategies are presented in Figure 6.1.

Title of Book: ____________________ Author: ____________________ This action takes place on pages __________	
What are Jeffrey's actions during this reading?	What do these actions tell you about this character?
What are John's actions during this reading?	What do these actions tell you about Jeffrey?
What are the actions of the other kids who are watching?	What do these actions tell you about Jeffrey?
What do you know about Jeffrey that you didn't know before you read this passage? ____________________	

Figure 6.4. Language chart on character analysis through actions.

The texts used during small group instruction are based on students' instructional reading levels. This differs from texts at a student's independent level—texts that can already be read independently—or texts at the frustrational level—texts that are so difficult that they will not likely be of instructional benefit. As Ivey and Fisher (2005) noted, the selected texts should also be interesting for students. It seems obvious, but students will not want to acquire comprehension strategies only to read texts that are boring!

The general flow of the small group guided comprehension strategy instruction lesson is as follows:

- Activate background knowledge or link with prior knowledge
- Introduce the text
- Model, if necessary, a comprehension strategy
- Establish a purpose for reading

- Ask students to read the text, often aloud but quietly so that the teacher can assess
- Discuss the text and invite students to explain how they used the strategy
- Praise students on the use of the target strategy
- During and after the lesson, record observation related to future instruction needed by individual students

During a small group session focused on comprehension strategy instruction, Arian's teacher reminded the group of the purpose they had set as a whole class. The big questions they discussed included the following:

- How does a person's race impact or influence the choices this person has in life?
- Has the impact of race changed over the past one hundred years?
- How much further do we have to go?

As a class, they were reading *Black Boy* (Wright, 1998). They had already written in their journals as part of one of the collaborative learning activities. The prompt on this particular day was:

> Do you know anyone who has been mistreated because of his or her race, religion, ethnicity, or some other personal characteristic?

The teacher focused on the literary element of mood during his whole class read-aloud of the text. As he read, he paused to provide students with more information about the mood. He said:

> Mood refers to the atmosphere [e.g., reflective, comic, etc.] that exists in a piece of writing. In other words, it is the overall attitude the reader gets from the reading. Authors use words to create the mood for their writing. The mood can be established by the author's use or non-use of humor, exaggeration, and word choice, to name a few.
>
> Most readers would say that the mood of the Richard Wright's autobiography is grave and serious. It follows the struggle and sufferings of a sensitive black man who tries to establish his identity in an unjust world. Richard has to deal with a number of hurdles before reaching his goal. As we read this text, pay attention to the words the author uses to establish the mood. Make a list of the words and phrases you identify as I read, and we'll discuss them after the reading.

During the small group instruction in which Arian was a member, the teacher knew that he needed to build additional background knowledge. The four students in this group and the teacher discussed the fact that the protections guaranteed under the U.S. Constitution were missing from the South during Richard Wright's early life. The teacher said:

> The Constitution clearly states that "all men are created equal," but in many places in the South back then, African Americans were continuously persecuted for things that would be acceptable in today's society. In the early twentieth century the South was a place of racial prejudice, discrimination, and hate; blacks could be punished for simply looking at a white person in the wrong way. Punishments including arrests, beatings; even lynchings were common.

The small group talked about these things and made connections between their journal entries and the background information their teacher provided. Arian commented, "it's not much different for today. People get mistreated because of they skin color." Following this discussion, which was designed to activate and build background knowledge, the teacher introduced some of Richard Wright's haiku poems (Wright, 1998). He asked the students to take a minute to read the poems aloud in their whisper voices so that he could hear their pronunciation, fluency, and prosody.

When they had each read through the haiku poems several times, with the teacher providing them with guidance on pronunciation and fluency, he stopped them and asked that they visualize the poems. He said, "What do you see in your minds? We know that this helps us understand, so let's take a minute to discuss what we see in our minds with a partner." He listened in, providing prompts and clues as necessary.

The teacher then turned the conversation to his focus on literary elements. He asked, "How would you describe the mood of each of these poems? Which words lead you to respond the way you did?" The discussion that followed allowed him to provide some direct instruction on mood and the author's choice of words to convey mood. The students in this group benefited from this focused interaction, which ensured that they were more prepared for the subsequent lessons on the text and the devices that were under investigation. As they left their small groups, the teacher provided their next writing prompt, which would become the topic of conversation for their next meeting. The prompt read, "Select one of the haiku above and compare it with *Black Boy*. How are the tones in these two works similar and different?"

Reciprocal Teaching

Reciprocal teaching allows students to use comprehension strategies in conversations with their peers. In essence, they become instructors of the content they are studying and engage one another in discussions about meaning. The four components of reciprocal teaching are summarizing, questioning, clarifying, and predicting (Palincsar, 1987).

This structured inquiry provides students with a process for exploring text and checking their own comprehension (Alfassi, 1998; Oczkus, 2003). In groups of four, students discuss with each other the content from a text. Typically, students take turns and rotate through each of the four components. The text is parsed, either by the teacher or by the students, and they stop periodically during the reading to discuss what they have read. The discussion focuses on the four components of reciprocal teaching.

When *summarizing*, the student focuses on the "big ideas" from the section of the text and shares them with the group. *Questions* are created by one of the students and then discussed or answered with the group. In the *clarifying* phase, the reader focuses on unfamiliar vocabulary and puzzling concepts or ideas. When clarifying, the student who focuses on that component shares his or her understanding and asks members of the group to share theirs. In the final component, *predicting*, the student uses all the information available in the reading, including pictures and text structure, to determine what might happen next. Over time, and with practice, students begin to incorporate these four comprehension strategies into their independent reading.

To be effective, reciprocal teaching requires that students first learn the process. Most English teachers model the type of thinking involved in each of the components of reciprocal teaching as part of their think-alouds (discussed earlier in this chapter). As students understand the types of comments they can make for each of the components, they are ready to use comments in collaborative learning situations. When groups of students first begin to use reciprocal teaching, we suggest that the teacher join in different groups and model the types of conversations he or she expects. During a twenty-minute reciprocal teaching lesson in which the entire class is working in groups of four, the teacher should be able to join the conversation in four or five groups. Once the groups are up and running, the teacher can meet with specific students in guided comprehension strategy instruction groups (see the previous section).

Abdurashid's twelfth-grade English teacher focused a significant amount of instructional time on expository reading and writing. She knows that success in college requires that students be able to read for information, write reports of information, and engage in nonfiction or informational texts. As one of their units of study, the class explored time management. To activate their background knowledge, the teacher began the class with a quick-write: "How do you spend your time?" Abdurashid wrote for about three minutes about going to school, studying, sleeping, playing sports, and eating. As students wrote, the teacher distributed a short article from *Newsweek* about the ways in which teens spend their time. They read the article and discussed it in groups of four using reciprocal teaching, taking turns summarizing, questioning, clarifying, and predicting.

During the first round, Abdurashid was the questioner. He asked his group three questions:

- How much time do teenagers spend on homework? Do you remember?
- How does this compare with your time use?
- What questions would you ask this reporter?

During the second round, Abdurashid was the predictor. His prediction focused on the idea that the reporter would suggest that teenagers were not using their time wisely. He also predicted that the reporter would say that teenagers needed more sleep.

The class read a number of articles over the next few days focusing on time management. The reciprocal teaching groups read some of the articles, the teacher read some articles aloud, and still others were used as choice readings for groups to select from. Over the two weeks that the class focused on time management and reading and writing for information, Abdurashid read or discussed four magazine articles, two newspaper articles, one scientific journal article, one essay, one poem, and a diary entry. He also analyzed graphs and charts and collected data on his own use of time. His final essay for this unit of study can be found in Figure 6.5.

Leadership in English

Comprehension in content area reading is a cornerstone of learning in the secondary classroom, and English teachers can assume a leadership role in schoolwide conversations about this topic. While content area colleagues are sensitive to the notion of turning into "reading teachers," we have found them to be excellent allies in promoting the use of literacy strategies in their courses. A first step toward this is to share in-

Time Budget Essay

Over seven days, I maintained a record of how I spent my time. This was a very important project for me as I was moving out of my father's house at the time and into my own apartment. It was good for me to have to analyze how I spent time, especially since I would have a lot less structure to my time when I lived in my own apartment. The assignment was given at the perfect time for me to think about budgeting my time to get my work done. If I were writing a newspaper article about this project, I would title it, "Teen Spends Too Much Time on Homework!"

However, this is not a newspaper article, it is a report and a reaction to the data and some additional readings from our groups. I will first discuss my reaction to the data I collected then I will comment on three things that I noticed when I first saw the data presented in a pie chart. I will conclude this paper by reacting to the additional readings provided in the information packet.

Reaction

Keeping on track of what I do all day and recording the time spent on each task wasn't as easy as it seemed. The main reason for this difficulty is that I am not used to such habit as recording my daily activities. At first I tried recording my activities every night before I went to bed. But that didn't work out much because I get overwhelmed when thinking about what I have been doing all day, especially some days are not good. Yet, I used this method for the first three days. Then I changed my method to an easier way of keeping my time log. I kept a little notebook in my pocket and every time I did something I would record the name of the activity and the time. This saved me time and additional stress that I began to reflect every night on what I recorded all day long. Despite some discomfort that this activity might bring to some beginners like me, it teaches very important lessons about life. It makes us realize how precious time is and gives us the opportunity to appreciate ourselves for how we use our time to do some valuable things in our everyday life. While doing the assignment, I always felt professional because I thought that I was demonstrating the ability of time management, which is key to success in life. Though I felt a little uneasy about this activity at the beginning, my reaction to it changed as I finished entering the data into my spreadsheet. It feels that everything I do is important when I see it recorded.

Three Observations

When I see my pie chart, three things really surprised me the moment I observe them. The time I spent sleeping, the time I spend in school, and especially the time I spend doing my homework and studying. The pie chart indicates that I spend the highest percentage of my life sleeping compared with other activities I do. The fact is that I have never gotten enough sleep in my life. The maximum number of hours I sleep is six, and it happens only once in a while. Yet, in the pie chart it surprised me when I saw that I spent more time sleeping than doing my other activities. The second surprise was the time I spent studying and doing my homework. Although I knew that I spent much of my time studying and doing my homework, I was shocked to discover that I spent 36% on academics.

continued on next page

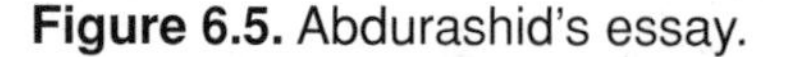
Figure 6.5. Abdurashid's essay.

Figure 6.5. continued

I was also surprised with the amount of time I spent exercising. Exercising is my favorite activity but I spent only total of 5% in a week doing this. Many things in our daily activities surprise us when we see them as a visual image. I drew the conclusion that I must of reconsider how I spend my time. Not that I waste my time everyday, but I realize I lack balance, which is very important for one's health both emotionally and physically.

Getting Enough Sleep

As I mentioned earlier, I have never gotten enough sleep, especially since I started high school. My average sleeping time is four hours. Almost everyday I go to bed at 1 or 2 AM. My issue of not getting too much sleep is not associated with my parents at all. My case is a little different. Since I came to this country, I established high expectation to accomplish the opportunities that are out there for whoever wanted to take advantage of them. I set a goal to learn English as fast as I could to be able to take advantage of these opportunities. So, I study many extra hours and think about my past, present and future a lot. Having this in my mind, it becomes almost impossible to go to bed and to sleep as peacefully as I should. I have to do all my work, study ahead of the class and reassure myself that I'm doing everything that I have to do to make it to the next level in my life; then my mind will be free and I will be able to sleep. This is not the only issue. I also miss my family back home in Ethiopia, especially my mother and my brothers and sisters and I think about them every night. Due to all of these problems, sleeping has never been easy to me.

"Teens, Sleep, and School"

The article did not change my answer. In fact, it taught me additional reasons for lack of sleep among teenagers. However, the article presents a completely different reason than mine for teens not having enough sleep. In the article it shows that some studies suggest, "teens experience a hormonal shift that affects their sleep patterns." Well, this may be true for many teens. But my case was not really the hormonal shift or anything, it was associated with my social life and personal experiences whose memories come every second and ring a wake-up bell in my ears. Regardless of that, I agree with the article that teenagers also experience biological changes in their bodies during their teenhood that might affect their sleeping pattern. It is just one of the many reasons that teens do not get enough sleep.

"Procrastination"

I can relate to this article. Procrastination for me is simply fear of being successful or fear of not being able to live up to others' or my own expectations. I can connect it to my study habits and everyday experiences in my school and classes. While in class, I have the habit of participating and doing my work as assigned unless I have very a difficult problem that might keep me from doing so. As I live by these habits, there are times when I experience a feeling or fear that is hard to explain. This

continued on next page

Figure 6.5. continued

feeling usually comes to me when when I encounter challenging class work, quizzes, or tests. Inside I think that my teacher thinks I am genius and know and understands most of the things she/he teaches. Having this idea in mind, when I get wrong answers in class I tend to experience a great deal of emabarrasement and will stop participating for the rest of the period, even for the next few days sometimes. During this period of time, I procrastinate because I start telling myself that I shouldn't show all my knowledge in class and that I should pretend like I don't know what's going on. This is a direct indicator of fear to succeed, fear to live up to mine and other's expectations. But, through my experiences I have learned that procrastination only makes things worse. The only way out is to face whatever is causing it. Although the article reminds me of myself, it also reminds me to be proud of myself at the same time by realizing that this is a common issue among many people and I don't have to worry about it anymore.

Conclusion

Doing this project helped me learn more about myself in a short period of time. The time log, the charts, and graphs have let me see myself in a more visible way than I have ever seen my life. It taught me the importance of keeping a record of not only my daily activities but also the many things that happen in my community everyday. By keeping a record, I will really know the community that I think I know now. Looking at my graphs and charts, one can conclude one thing about me. The most important thing in my life that I spent most of my time on is my education. The time I spend in school and the time I spend studying and doing my homework says a lot about my education and me. My parents may think that they know me more than anyone else, yet if they see these graphs and chart I am sure they would be surprised. Maybe they would even be proud of me or worry about me. I spend most of my time in my school and studying because I value education more than anything in this life.

formation about the comprehension strategies being taught in the English classrooms, so that they can utilize the strategies as needed in their own teaching. A primary purpose for raising the knowledge level of content area colleagues on comprehension strategies is so that they can think aloud for their students.

Think-alouds are one of the most effective instructional strategies used with content reading material. In our work with teachers, we stress the importance of their own expertise as readers and consumers of information about science, mathematics, history, and the arts. Therefore, we ask them to think aloud as a scientist, a mathematician, a historian, an artist—not as an English teacher. Think-alouds in the hands of a content area expert give English language learners insight into how informational text is understood within the context of the subject.

Since textbooks can be challenging for many secondary students, reciprocal teaching can be a useful strategy for promoting comprehension of content area materials. The English department can assume a leadership role in teaching students about reciprocal teaching so that content area colleagues can use it in their classrooms. Teachers at Hoover developed a simple set of procedures and prompts on reciprocal teaching, taught it in the English classes, and then shared these materials with the rest of the staff.

Leadership in comprehension instruction can also come in the form of independent reading. As noted in Chapter 3, time for independent reading of content materials is an excellent strategy for boosting vocabulary and background knowledge. This is also a good time to remind colleagues that independent reading in their classrooms provides English language learners with opportunities to apply the comprehension strategies they have learned in English in order to further their learning in their other courses.

Conclusion

> Neither comprehension nor learning can take place in an atmosphere of anxiety. (Rose Kennedy)

Comprehension is viewed as the "gold standard" for reading and can pose a significant barrier for English language learners who are being challenged to learn a new language and the content simultaneously. However, as Rose Kennedy noted, students need to feel comfortable while learning and comprehending. Sound instruction involves utilizing these strategies as the text demands, yet they are often mistakenly taught in isolation. The "cooperation of forces" needed to understand text is best taught through teacher modeling, guided instruction, and peer collaboration so that English language learners are able to comprehend at increasingly independent levels. Comprehension involves all the elements discussed in this book, including grammar, fluency, and vocabulary.

7 The English Classroom: A Place for Language Learning

In the previous chapters, we have examined a variety of strategies for developing language and literacy of English language learners in English classrooms. We have examined the theory and rationale for using these strategies, along with the unique challenges for English language learners. The strategies are easy to implement and highly engaging for students. Without considering the end goal, however, they are much like the groceries in your cupboard. You can have a well-stocked pantry, full of gourmet goods, but without a recipe, they are nothing more than a list of ingredients, perhaps inviting but perhaps inedible unless combined with suitable items. Similarly, without a conceptual framework for organizing instruction, the best strategies, while comprising an admirable repertoire of activities, may not move our students further along the journey to academic proficiency. Without knowing our students and knowing where we are going, we cannot use these strategies strategically. Individually, the strategies in this book may make learning more fun, but without organizing them in ways that allow students to construct meaning and gain increasing independence, they will not significantly raise achievement.

At the same time, we cannot dissect language and learning to the point that it becomes meaningless, disconnected from the lived experiences of our students. We are reminded of the cautionary tale by nonsense writer Edward Lear (1812–1888), who wrote:

> A centipede was happy quite,
> Until a frog in fun
> Said, "Pray, which leg comes after which?"
> This raised her mind to such a pitch,
> She lay distracted in the ditch
> Considering how to run.

We hope that by providing a framework for purposeful planning that incorporates research-based learning approaches and utilizes a gradual release of responsibility model of instruction, teachers will not lay distracted in a ditch wondering what to do for their English language learners.

It is also important to recognize the differences between teaching ELL students and teaching other struggling readers and writers, including standard English learners. The approaches and strategies discussed in this book are certainly effective and appropriate for virtually all students. The differences for English language learners lie primarily in four areas: the amount of scaffolding needed, the emphasis on vocabulary and language structure, the amount of time needed to engage in oral language practice, and the focus on building background knowledge. In our planning we must be sure to do the following:

Provide Additional Scaffolding. Although all our students benefit from purposeful scaffolding and teacher support, students who are learning a new language at the same time as they are learning new content may need more modeling and guided practice than their native English-speaking peers before they are ready to work independently. One or two scaffolded tasks may suffice for native English speakers, where English language learners may need four or five to reach the same level of competency. The "message abundancy" (Gibbons, 2003) and language redundancy offered by the additional scaffolding allow English language learners the time they need to process, practice, and understand high levels of academic language and content.

Emphasize Vocabulary and Language Structure. While all our students need to learn a massive amount of vocabulary, as we saw in Chapter 3, English language learners begin their secondary schooling with a significantly smaller vocabulary that often does not include many words easily understood by native English-speakers. And both standard English learners and English language learners will need explicit instruction on grammatical structures.

Provide Time for Oral Language Practice. Although all our students benefit from engaging in active discussion of concepts, English language learners need this time to practice language as well as expanding their use of academic English as they negotiate and clarify meaning with others.

Build Background Knowledge. While all our students, at different times, will need time to build background knowledge to prepare them for the complex ideas and skills that are the focus of the secondary English language arts standards, as we discussed in Chapter 2, our English language learners may lack some of the background we take for granted because of missed schooling, or schooling in another country, or simply different experiences.

A Framework for Effective Teaching of English Language Learners

Effective teaching for English language learners can be organized into three phases of instruction: preparing to learn, interacting with text, and extending the learning (WestEd, 2002a). This model for planning is based on a sociocultural theory of learning that provides a conceptual framework within which we can develop academic language and build student understanding and independence.

The approaches we have discussed throughout this book—encompassing vocabulary development, grammar instruction, fluency building, and teaching for comprehension—fit easily into this framework. Thus strategies such as think-alouds, shared reading, generative sentences, and reciprocal teaching become the tools used by teachers to ensure that students are prepared for learning, that they interact with text, and that they extend and apply their learning. Table 7.1 illustrates how the learning approaches identified by NCTE are implemented within the phases of instruction—preparing, interacting, and extending.

Key to effective teaching is gradually releasing responsibility for learning from the teacher to the student. As discussed in Chapter 2, this provides English language learners with purposefully scaffolded experiences that allow them to assume progressively more control of their learning as they apply the skills and strategies modeled by the teacher. Figure 7.1 demonstrates the relationship between the gradual release model, the conceptual framework, and effective instructional approaches for ELL students. As teachers move through the three phases of instruction—preparing, interacting, extending—they gradually release an increasing amount of responsibility to the students. It is important to note that this model is not entirely linear—within each phase of instruction teachers are constantly monitoring and adjusting the level of support according to student need and progress. During the preparation phase of a lesson, students must be expected to take responsibility for their own learning, just as during the extension of learning phase teachers must scaffold the tasks as needed. And neither is the construct of preparing, interacting, and extending an entirely linear process. It may be that even as students are extending their learning from a text, they are engaged in preparing to interact with a new text; or the lesson sequence may move back and forth between preparing and interacting before students apply their learning.

Table 7.1. The Role of English Teachers in Educating English Language Learners

Phase of Instruction	Learning Approaches
Preparing to Learn	■ Connect the reading with the students' background/cultural knowledge and experiences ■ Encourage students to talk about their background knowledge in relation to the topic ■ Have students read a more accessible text on the topic first ■ Ask families to read with students a version of the text in the heritage language ■ Read aloud frequently to allow students to become familiar with and appreciate the sounds and structures of written language ■ Introduce key vocabulary ■ Stimulate students' content knowledge of the text before introducing the text
Interacting with Text	■ Encourage students to discuss the readings, including the cultural dimensions of the text ■ Teach language features—text structure, vocabulary, and text- and sentence-level grammar ■ Teach key vocabulary essential for the topic ■ Deconstruct (chunk ideas and reading) and reconstruct (create schema) the text ■ Encourage students to discuss the readings ■ Encourage students to take a critical stance ■ Teach text- and sentence-level grammar in context to help students understand the text ■ Teach the specific features of language students need to communicate about the text
Extending the Learning	■ Provide experiences in writing to clarify understanding of reading ■ Encourage students to discuss the readings ■ Provide opportunities for students to apply new learning to new situations

Source: Adapted from *Position Paper on the Role of English Teachers in Educating English Language Learners (ELLs)*, by National Council of Teachers of English, 2006 (Urbana, IL: Author), and "Teacher Professional Development," by WestEd, 2003, handout from Quality Teaching for English Learners Building the Base Institute, July 2006.

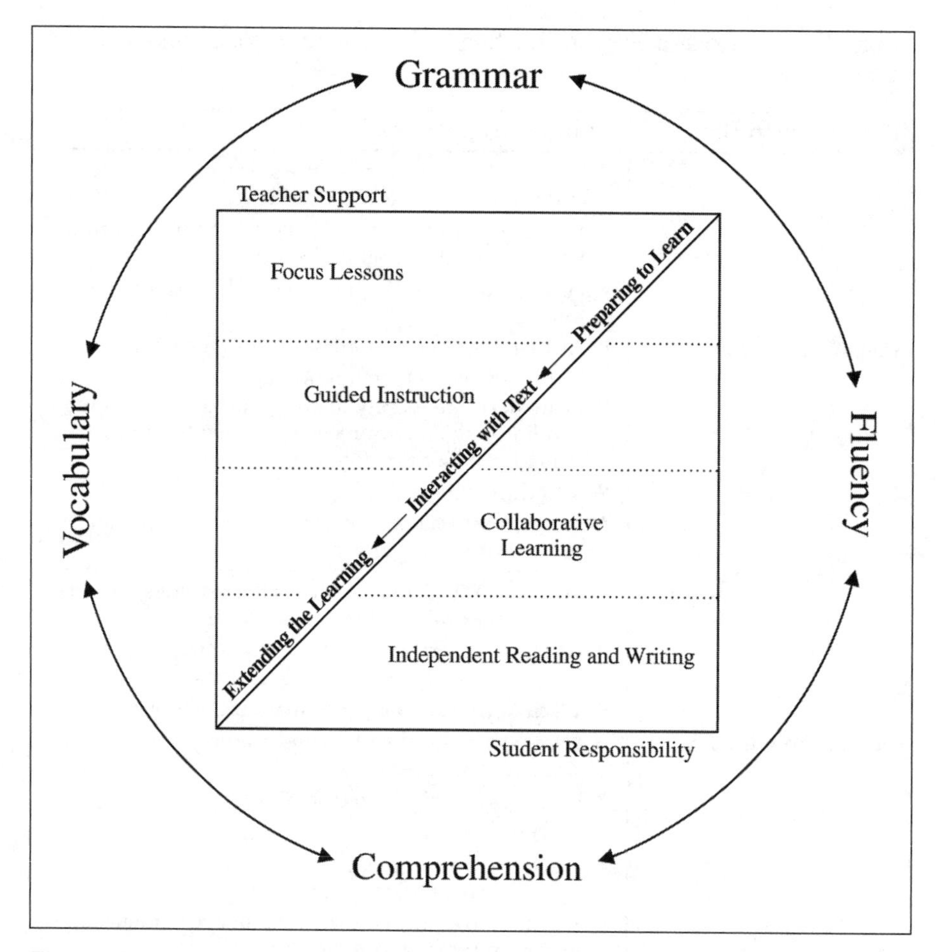

Figure 7.1. Research-based approaches applied within a conceptual framework that prepares, provides interaction, and extends learning through a gradual release of responsibility model.

Planning: Preparing to Learn

The initial lessons in a unit of study, and the first part of each lesson, are critical to setting the context and focusing students' attention on the key concepts or skills you want them to learn. This is an element of planning that can often be overlooked or at best done superficially in our efforts to address all the standards and keep pace with the curriculum map of the school. It is, however, a critical part of the lesson that gets students "ready to learn," activates prior knowledge, sets expectations and a purpose for learning, and provides them with a "map" of where they are headed. Effective readers and learners automatically activate prior knowledge and set a purpose for interacting with text or with others. They employ a variety of strategies to make meaning of unknown vocabulary. They ask questions of themselves, of others, and of the text, in order to clarify understanding. Effective teachers recognize that they must facilitate this process for many of their students—providing them with information and tools they need to develop deep levels of understanding along with the language skills needed to express that understanding. This is the phase of instruction where we activate prior knowledge, set the purpose, and introduce vocabulary.

Activate Prior Knowledge. Asking students to bring their personal experiences or prior learning into play helps them connect new learning to that which they already know, preparing them to build schema and expand their understanding. We know that the brain processes parts and wholes simultaneously (Zadina, 2004), so as students learn the parts, they must also see the whole picture to understand how the parts fit together. As Henry Adams noted, "All experience is an arch to build upon."

Set the Purpose. Setting the purpose helps students focus their attention on the important ideas of the lesson. When students know the purpose of the lesson, they can "focus on what is important instead of what is unusual" (Hill & Flynn, 2006, p. 48). When teachers are clear about their purpose, it helps to keep them on track toward the new knowledge or skills they want their students to develop. Setting the purpose goes beyond telling the students what they are going to *do* that day; rather it is telling them what they are expected to *learn* that day in a way that lets them know what they should be looking and listening for. "We are going to see how the words an author uses can help us identify their bias"—rather than "Today we are going to read an editorial" or even "Today we are going to learn about bias."

Introduce Vocabulary. Preparing to learn may entail introducing or pre-teaching vocabulary as a way to facilitate access to the texts. Words selected for pre-teaching should be necessary for understanding the key content and ones that students will have multiple opportunities to use and practice throughout the unit of study. They should be presented in context, not as a list of words with definitions to look for while reading.

Learning Approaches for Preparing to Learn. There are a number of effective learning approaches for preparing to learn, including the following:

- Advance organizers
- Question answering
- Question generating
- Graphic organizers
- Read-alouds
- Think-alouds
- Words of the Week

Preparing to Learn Using a Gradual Release of Responsibility Model. Keep in mind that while the beginning of a unit of study is focused on preparing to learn, the delivery of instruction is not limited to modeling alone. A major goal in this initial phase is for students to learn to activate their own prior and background knowledge. Consider how a middle school English teacher uses a gradual release model to get students ready to learn. Note how the approaches to vocabulary, fluency, grammar, and comprehension that we have discussed in previous chapters are woven into the fabric of the lessons.

- **Focus Lesson:** The teacher reads aloud a passage on the Dust Bowl from her students' American history textbook to build background knowledge on this era.

  Fluency: She can read the passage a second time to model fluent reading, asking students to pay attention to *how* she reads—utilizing punctuation, phonemic awareness, and so on.

  Vocabulary: At this time she highlights some of the key vocabulary she will expect students to learn and use. She also uses this as an opportunity to make transparent the processes she uses to approach unfamiliar words. This is a good time to help students recognize any cognates that occur in the text.
- **Guided Instruction:** Students at similar levels of English language proficiency meet with the teacher to read and discuss an advance organizer about texts set in the Dust Bowl era. These include *The Grapes of Wrath* (Steinbeck, 1939), which will be used as a shared reading for the entire class, as well as *Out of the Dust* (Hesse, 1997) and *No Promises in the Wind* (Hunt, 2002), the two independent readings for the class. Students will eventually read one of these books as part of their unit of study.

  Comprehension: The advance organizer helps to build comprehension through providing a schema for students. It is also an opportunity to build additional background knowledge during the discussion. The teacher spends time teaching students the strategy of using an advance organizer to guide their reading and improve comprehension. She shows them how to use it to monitor their understanding as they read.

Vocabulary: The advance organizer contains some of the key vocabulary in the unit, and the teacher uses this opportunity to provide additional instruction on this vocabulary.

- **Collaborative Learning:** Based on what they have learned thus far, students work in pairs to compose a set of inquiry questions for the unit. The questions are posted on a class chart and are referenced throughout the unit.

  Grammar: This is a good time to provide English language learners with question frames to help them formulate their questions using correct grammatical structures.

- **Independent Reading and Writing:** Each student engages in a brief writing to learn activity to summarize the information they have learned through the introduction of the Dust Bowl–era information and the previewing activity with the books for the unit. The teacher reads these short summaries to gain a sense of what the students have retained and what misconceptions might need to be clarified before proceeding with the unit of study.

  Grammar: Through this writing the teacher can identify specific aspects of language structure to target for a mini-lesson with small groups of ELL students.

  Fluency: Writing to learn provides contextualized opportunities for students to build writing fluency. This can be done as a Power Write where students are given three one-minute opportunities to write what they have learned.

Planning: Interacting with Text

This is the phase where students increase their factual knowledge, develop conceptual understanding, and practice the academic language needed to talk about that understanding. It is important that we recognize the interdependence of this factual knowledge and the overall conceptual framework. Being able to define racism (factual knowledge) allows students reading *Black Boy* to explain (using academic language) how Richard Wright's perspective on race influenced his writing (conceptual understanding). Students' ability to identify a variety of rhetorical devices such as irony, metaphors, and similes (factual knowledge) allows them to analyze (using academic language) an author's implicit and explicit philosophical assumptions and beliefs about a subject (conceptual understanding). In Shakespeare's *Julius Caesar*, students must be able to explain what irony is, as well as how and why irony is used by Mark Antony in the statement, "Yet Brutus says he was ambitious; / And Brutus is an honourable man" (act 3, scene 2).

As students interact with text and with the concept, they engage in three primary functions: deconstructing the text, building schema, and, finally, taking a critical stance (WestEd 2002a). (Here again, the distinctions in the phases of instruction are somewhat blurred as taking a critical stance might also be an extension of learning.)

Deconstruct the Text. Chunking the text and analyzing each chunk facilitates development of both factual knowledge and conceptual understanding. Deconstructing the text can mean developing vocabulary, practicing a grammatical structure, summarizing information, or interpreting the author's purpose. Analyzing the parts of a text builds the understanding students need in order to take a critical stance or formulate their own response to the text.

Build Schema. As students gain new understanding they build on existing schema, connecting the new ideas and skills to their prior knowledge. As they analyze and develop understanding of each chunk of text, they are able to connect the ideas to fit into the whole.

Take a Critical Stance. Interacting with text means just that—to act together (interact, n.d., *WordNet*), collaborate, combine, connect (interact, n.d., *Roget's*). It is not a passive event, but rather a two-way process where the learner reads, listens, and responds. Students negotiate and construct meaning as they challenge a persuasive message, critique the logic of a functional document, or evaluate the credibility of an author's argument.

Learning Approaches for Interacting with Text. There are a number of effective strategies for helping students interact with text, including the following:

- Wide reading
- Graphic organizers
- Shared reading
- Reciprocal teaching
- Generative sentences
- Sentence combining
- Sentence syntax surgery
- Fluency practice
- Power Writing

Interacting with Text Using a Gradual Release of Responsibility Model

This phase is the heart of the unit of study and the time in which teachers are building standards-based knowledge. The gradual release of responsibility model of instruction is used throughout so that students become increasingly independent in their application of factual and conceptual knowledge. In the following scenario, a high school teacher uses a gradual release model to facilitate student interaction with texts. At the same time, students are using new vocabulary, building fluency, practicing grammar, and applying comprehension strategies.

- **Focus Lesson:** The teacher uses a think-aloud process to analyze a passage from *The Grapes of Wrath* to model how she arrives at an understanding of the symbolism of the turtle's struggle to cross a desolate section of highway in Chapter 3 as a metaphor for the struggle faced by the Joad family and others escaping the Dust Bowl.

  Vocabulary: She also models how she uses context clues, knowledge of word parts, rereading, and so on to understand unfamiliar vocabulary.
- **Guided Instruction:** The teacher meets with a small group of students who are reading *Out of the Dust* to discuss the symbolism of the burns on Billie Jo's hands and her inability to play the piano because of them.

  Vocabulary: This is an opportunity to highlight the vocabulary the author uses to show the symbolism. Students might complete a semantic feature analysis or do a word sort to engage in meaningful ways with the new vocabulary.

  Grammar: The teacher can also point out language structures that have been the focus of instruction. They might do some sentence syntax surgery with some of the sentences from the text.
- **Collaborative Learning:** Pairs of students reading *Out of the Dust* and *No Promises in the Wind* read aloud passages of their choosing from their books to one another and explain why they found it meaningful.

  Fluency: This provides fluency practice in a low-risk environment and allows students to summarize and explain the content of the book to someone who is not familiar with the story. As the partners work, the teacher can read with individual students using the Neurological Impress Method (see Chapter 5).

  Comprehension: Students can use reciprocal teaching to build their comprehension.
- **Independent Reading and Writing:** Students read newspaper accounts of the time selected by their teacher from *Americans View Their Dust Bowl Experience* (Wunder, Kaye, & Carstensen, 2001) and then write a précis about the article.

  Grammar: Teachers can use sentence and/or paragraph frames and individual conferring to support English language learners as they write. The teacher can assign different students to write to a different audience in a different format and then lead a follow-up discussion that helps students recognize the different ways that we express the same ideas depending on the context (contrastive rhetoric).

Planning: Extending the Learning

Knowledge and understanding without application is about as useful as owning a bicycle without ever using it—it is only through actually riding that we learn to ride a bicycle, just as it is only through using, or applying, new learning that students expand schema and develop independence. This third phase of learning occurs when we ask students to apply their new knowledge in relation to the whole. They cement their knowledge and deepen their understanding by using the new learning to analyze, evaluate, and elaborate. There are two key elements to this process.

Apply New Learning. Once students have developed factual knowledge and understanding of ideas, they are ready to engage at the higher levels of Bloom's taxonomy, especially applying, analyzing, synthesizing, and evaluating the new concepts. They can use their new understanding to create a product, conduct original analysis, or take a critical stance expressing their own perspective. In a unit on reading informational text, they might take a position on a ballot measure and then write an editorial expressing that position. Arian's understanding of Richard Wright's perspective in *Black Boy* allowed her to analyze recurrent themes about the cruelty of racism and the conflict of an individual versus society, connecting her own perspective to Wright's. Arian selected the following quote on which to write an essay that illustrated two themes: "The naked will to power seemed always to walk in the wake of a hymn" (Wright, 1998, p. 136). She explained her choice:

> I chose this quote because I saw how Richard's life was filled with beatings "for his own good." His mother and aunt would beat him and then tell him that he needed to follow his religion's teachings. He grew strong inside even as he turned away from his church. He used that strength to fight against racism in the American society. There are many times when a person draws strength from their religion. But if their religion is used to punish, it can make a person reject their beliefs. People can draw strength from believing strongly in something, or by rejecting those beliefs.

Reflect on Learning. Reflection is a powerful way to release an increasing amount of responsibility to students as they self-monitor and set goals for their own learning. Students can do quick writes as a writing-to-learn activity, talk with a partner, or complete a learning log. Many English teachers use self-assessment to ask students to reflect on their learning in relation to the stated purpose of the lesson, in relation to other subject areas, or in relation to their own lives. As they think about what they have learned, they can analyze how it fits into other learning (schema) and evaluate how well they learned, recognize what strategies they used that helped them, and identify what they need to work on next (metacognition).

Learning Approaches for Extending the Learning. Effective strategies that have been discussed in this book for extending the learning include the following:

- Reciprocal teaching
- Question generating
- Writing to learn
- Readers theater
- Wide reading

Extending the Learning Using a Gradual Release of Responsibility Model

In many ways, this is the most challenging phase because the focus is on moving students beyond recall of information to develop critical literacy as they examine representation, themes of social justice, and bias by questioning the author and the message. Students use narrative and informational texts to expand their worldviews by integrating what they have learned into their existing knowledge and experiences. Here we show how the same high school teacher uses a gradual release model to extend her students' understanding of literary devices as well as the social issues that provided the impetus for the message in *The Grapes of Wrath*. Note how students continue to practice vocabulary, fluency, grammar, and comprehension strategies in this phase.

- **Focus Lesson:** The teacher models her own writing processes by showing students her first draft of a persuasive essay written to President Franklin Delano Roosevelt on the needs of the Joad family and then by making revisions to her work as they watch.

  Vocabulary and Grammar: She highlights vocabulary and language structures that help to persuade the reader. Students can add new words to their vocabulary journals.

- **Guided Instruction:** Small groups of similarly achieving students meet with the teacher to read their drafts to one another, based on the characters in the novels they read. Students listen and provide feedback, while the teacher provides guidance in effective methods for peer responses.

  Vocabulary and Grammar: The teacher spends additional time with ELL students, guiding their writing, focusing on language structure, discourse, and vocabulary. They might practice sentence combining or write generative sentences using the new vocabulary they are learning. As students give each other feedback on their writing, they can use sentence starters such as "When you wrote____, it really helped me understand your message. "

Fluency: Students practice reading aloud to each other with ease, expression, and correct pronunciation. Repeated reading of their text reinforces their fluency. Sentence starters also promote oral fluency as students discuss their writing. They not only support students in using standard academic English, but they teach culturally acceptable ways of participating in discussions. An added benefit is that they encourage students to conduct their conversations in English.

Comprehension: As students re-present the text in their writing, they deepen their understanding through analyzing and synthesizing their reading and applying their learning.

- **Collaborative Learning:** Students work in groups to practice sections of dialogue from either *Out of the Dust* or *No Promises in the Wind.* They discuss intonation, pronunciation, and phrase boundaries as they rehearse. All the groups will perform in a readers theater activity later in the week.

  Fluency: Readers theater is a particularly valuable way to develop fluency when students know that they are expected to read aloud with ease, expression, and correct pronunciation and have adequate opportunity to practice.

- **Independent Reading and Writing:** Students revisit the questions they generated at the beginning of this unit of study and check to see how many they can now answer. Unanswered questions are compiled and then analyzed by the class to determine which questions might be addressed to the history professor from the local university who will be a guest speaker the following week.

  Grammar: This is an opportunity for the teacher to confer with students about both their understanding of the content as well as their use of grammatical structures as they write answers to the questions.

  Comprehension: Revisiting their initial questions gives students an opportunity to monitor their learning.

Putting It All Together: A Glimpse inside the Classroom

We can accelerate the achievement of our English language learners through purposefully planned instruction that prepares them to interact with concepts and text and requires that they extend and apply their understanding. Using research-based learning approaches within and throughout, a gradual release of responsibility model of instruction provides the scaffolding necessary to achieve grade-level standards. Multiple opportunities to develop vocabulary, practice grammar, increase fluency, and utilize a variety of comprehension strategies are built into each element of this unit of study. Let's look at how these principles are applied in a ninth-grade English classroom.[1]

The content focus of this unit of instruction is on learning about literary devices featured in narrative texts and how readers analyze them to understand the meaning of the text. The language focus of the unit is on using vocabulary and grammatical structures to express their understanding of literary devices. The understanding is further extended as students use the literary devices in their own original writing. Any number of literary devices can be taught this way, including foreshadowing, flashbacks, and symbolism. Picture books and comics are used to model analysis of the focus elements. Students then use the software program Comic Life to create their own comics featuring literary devices taught in the class. (See http://plasq.com/ for more information about this inexpensive and award-winning software program.) The visual support from the picture books and comics scaffolds the learning for English language learners in a variety of ways—by making abstract concepts concrete, providing context for the story, and limiting dependence on language to make meaning. Graphic text provides that same support for informational text as well as narrative. Students can create their own graphic text to scaffold understanding of the structure of a piece of informational text by drawing a picture of each portion of the text. In reverse sequence, they can take a graphic text such as *The 9/11 Report* (Jacobson & Colón, 2006) and rewrite it in paragraph format.

Lesson Objectives

- Identify literary devices used in texts, such as metaphors, mood, tone, plot structures, symbolism, irony
- Incorporate identified literary devices in original writing
- Compose an essay on the use of literary devices in a piece of literature

Language Objectives

- Use phrases such as *when . . . , for example, the author's use of . . . , causes the reader to . . .* to explain how a literary device is used.
- Identify vocabulary used to enhance the effect of the literary device.

- Demonstrate subject-verb agreement.

Preparing to Learn

- **Focus Lesson:** Begin by introducing the literary device(s) selected for this unit. For example, the literary device of foreshadowing involves techniques the author uses to provide clues to an event that will occur later in the story. Explain that readers look for details that may suggest a future plot turn. In addition, readers pause during the reading to recall previous clues that may have first seemed insignificant but now have taken on importance. Authors use a number of techniques to foreshadow, including dialogue that reveals a character trait, describing the behavior of one or more characters, a plot turn that alters the circumstances for a character, or a brief setting change that divulges information that will become crucial later in the story. Playing a piece of the soundtrack from a popular movie that uses music to foreshadow an event is an engaging way to contextualize this concept. Remember Steven Spielberg's *Jaws* (1975)?

  The Caldecott Award–winning picture book *Tuesday* by David Wiesner (1991) is an ideal example of foreshadowing. Introduce this wordless picture book to the students, displaying the illustrations. The first page sets the stage: "Tuesday evening, around eight." Read each page with students, looking for the ways in which the illustrator foreshadows a strange event that is about to occur. The second page consists of three panels, zooming in on a scene of a turtle sitting on a log, eyes turned to the sky in alarm.

- **Guided Instruction:** Continue reading each page with the students, pointing out where foreshadowing is occurring. In a few pages they will understand that flying frogs are up to minor mischief in the local town. Once you finish reading the book, read *Tuesday* together again, this time asking students to identify the ways in which the author-illustrator foreshadowed events in the story. Compare these to the ways in which a writer uses techniques to foreshadow in prose text.

  Fluency: In small group guided instruction, students can practice oral fluency as they retell the story multiple times.

  Comprehension: Charting this process on a graphic organizer provides a visual reference for students, especially useful for English language learners who can easily forget ideas that are presented only orally, or who may have had difficulty tracking the conversation.

- **Collaborative Learning:** Now that students are comfortable with the literary device and techniques used, give them examples of other comics or excerpts from graphic novels that contain similar techniques. Invite students to work together to select a comic or graphic novel excerpt and discuss the literacy device(s) used. Ask them to compose a written summary of the story, with the attached comic. Remind students that they will create their own visual narrative using a software program. A jigsaw approach to this work allows the teacher to differentiate the level of support by assigning students to work in homogeneous "expert" groups where the teacher can provide additional guidance to small groups of ELL students as they compose an explanation of the literary device in their comic. Students can then return to heterogeneous "home" groups where they must explain their example to the rest of the group. Two excellent teacher resources are both by Will Eisner, often called "the grandfather of graphic novels." *Graphic Storytelling and Visual Narrative* (1996) and *Comics and Sequential Art* (1985) both feature detailed explanations of the techniques used in visual narratives and how they are linked to prose novels.

Vocabulary: The teacher can help students identify vocabulary that enhances the foreshadowing of their story.

Grammar and Comprehension: Sentence or paragraph frames are a useful guide to correct grammatical and textual structure.

Fluency: Students rehearse their explanations in their expert group before they explain it in their home group.

- **Independent Reading and Writing:** Invite students to write an explanatory paragraph on the literary device they will be using in their visual narrative. Remind them that the summary should include the name and definition of the literary device they have chosen, as well as an example from literature. There may be English language learners who will have difficulty completing this task independently. Additional modeling and shared writing in a small group setting can provide the necessary scaffolding.

  Vocabulary and Grammar: Paragraph frames and a list of vocabulary to include provide a bridge to academic writing.

Interacting with Text

- **Focus Lesson:** Use a data projector to show students how to use the Comic Life software program. Users need only a collection of digital photographs such as those stored electronically in iPhoto. Visual narratives are easily composed using this program because users can select the grid pattern (including number of frames needed), design dialogue boxes, and apply artistic treatments to the selected photos to create a visual narrative in comic form.
- **Guided Instruction:** Construct a simple comic using Comic Life with students. Ask them to make decisions about the storyline as well as the formatting.

Comprehension: A graphic organizer such as a storyboard helps ELL students to plan the structure of the text.

Fluency: The storyboard can include appropriate signal or joining words to scaffold the task of creating cohesive and grammatically accurate text.

- **Collaborative Learning:** Over one or two class periods, ask students to work in pairs to review digital photos and construct a story using the literary device you have been teaching. Students should produce a visual narrative that features the device, along with a written summary of the story. Again, the small group or partner structure allows the teacher to provide additional guidance or modeling for those who need it.

  Vocabulary and Grammar: It is helpful to provide ELL students with an example that highlights linking or signal words, subject-verb agreement, or other targeted language structures.

- **Independent Reading and Writing:** Provide students with a research library of materials in the classroom for constructing visual narratives, including *Comics and Sequential Art* (Eisner, 1985), *Graphic Storytelling and Visual Narrative* (Eisner, 1996), and *The Bristol Board Jungle* (Pendarvis & Kneece, 2004).

  We have included a visual narrative entitled "Black and White," written for a lesson on foreshadowing by two of our students using the Comic Life program (see Figure 7.2). Note that the students used dialogue to provide clues about the subject in panels 1–3, followed by a scene change in panel 4 that features a black-and-white animal print. Panel 5 switches back to the original setting, but it is only in the final panel that it becomes apparent that what caused the white and spotted cats' alarm was the presence of a black cat. As our students explained to us, "People stop and whisper sometimes when we're walking in a neighborhood where there's not a lot of African Americans and Latinos. We can spot the clues early, like foreshadowing. Those clues tell us what we can expect."

  Grammar: This is an opportunity to pull a small group and show English language learners how to write effective dialogue.

Extending the Learning

- **Focus Lesson:** Extend students' understanding of literary devices by returning students to traditional text. Select a short reading that exemplifies the literary device selected for this unit and conduct a think-aloud focused on how a reader understands the significance of the technique.

  Vocabulary: Underline and chart key words and phrases used by the author.

- **Guided Instruction:** Meet with small groups of students to discuss the novel, short story, or informational text they are read-

Figure 7.2. Black and White. Reprinted with permission of Benjamin Towle.

ing for class. Invite students to identify instances when the author used the same literary device (e.g., Langston Hughes's use of flashback in the short story "Thank You, M'am"). Encourage students to collect notes on this evidence and explain that they will develop an essay discussing these points.

Comprehension: A graphic organizer can help ELL students to track the structure of the text and focus on identifying the literary devices.

- **Collaborative Learning:** Ask students to meet in pairs to further develop their essays. Encourage them to provide feedback to one another on their draft essays.

  Vocabulary and Grammar: This is an opportunity to teach English language learners the sociolinguistic patterns of language that are typically used to provide feedback to peers.

  Vocabulary and Comprehension: Together students can create a concept chart to solidify their understanding of literary devices, use relevant academic vocabulary, and prepare them to write their essay.

- **Independent Reading and Writing:** Students work independently to make revisions to their literary device essays.

  Fluency: Students can read their essays aloud with a partner.

  Grammar: The teacher can work with individual students to help them understand where they may be transferring structures from their own language that do not transfer directly.

Students who participated in this unit of study on literary devices were first prepared by building background knowledge on the topic using picture books and graphic novels. They then worked together and independently to create an original visual narrative using a software program designed for ease of use. Only after they had created original compositions did they analyze prose texts for the same literary devices. Traditional instruction in the English classroom would begin with those time-honored texts, and many English language learners would likely struggle with attempting to reconcile abstract concepts (literary devices) with complex text written in a language they have not yet mastered. In contrast, this framework introduces an abstract concept with materials that lower the textual demand (through use of picture books) so that they can concentrate on the device. Students then apply the device in their original work (visual narratives). Only then are they ready to analyze the work of other authors and compose essays on the topic. Throughout the process, students are focused on building vocabulary, developing fluency, and practicing grammar, even as they learn how recognizing literary devices can deepen their comprehension.

Organizing the Day

The large majority of the strategies outlined in previous chapters in this book can be integrated directly into this or any other unit of study. There are two strategies, however, that merit their own dedicated time in the daily schedule: Words of the Week (WOW) and Sustained Silent Reading (SSR). Clearly, attention to word parts can and should be addressed in context whenever targeted roots and affixes appear in the text. The text alone, however, does not typically lend itself well to sustained and focused direct instruction. A WOW program that occupies a set time and sequence within the day's and week's instruction provides students with the variety of word parts as well as the practice necessary to accelerate the acquisition of academic vocabulary. SSR, for obvious reasons, must be a time for students to read text of their own choice at their own level. The texts they choose will likely not be related to the focus of instruction, and so this reading for enjoyment and stamina should also take place at a regular, predetermined, daily time.

Student Response and Teacher Feedback

We have focused significant attention in this book on the instructional moves that teachers make to ensure that students learn. We would be remiss if we did not also comment on the importance of student response patterns and how teachers can provide feedback that advances learning. A key component of effective feedback is having a clear understanding of the factors that contribute to the student's response. Mohr and Mohr (2007) have examined the variety of responses that we typically receive from ELL students and suggest that teachers can promote greater participation and learning through the reaction and feedback they provide. Figure 7.3 describes how consideration to these contributing factors can help us accomplish this.

Conclusion

The processes used in educating English language learners are the same effective tools for teaching all students. However, we recognize that language learners are more vulnerable to teaching practices that fail to account for their need for background knowledge, scaffolded instruction, and peer interactions. Teaching English language learners in the English classroom requires a paradigm shift regarding how we view students, texts, and learning.

Responses that are correct—Although praise is an appropriate response to correct answers, teachers should encourage English language learners to tell more, elaborate, or explain their answers, especially if the question elicits low-level thinking, such as recall, yes or no items, or conformational queries. Teachers should also confirm that students' use of English is effective.

Responses that are partially correct—Partially correct answers provide the teacher with an opportunity to assist students as they hone thinking, clarify knowledge, and accommodate information into their schemata, particularly in areas where prior knowledge is limited.

Response in a language other than English—Use of home language in the classroom should be viewed as evidence of student interest and willingness to transact with the lesson. Studies have shown that "other language" use is largely on task. Even when language learners whisper to one another, it is usually an effort to explain what the teacher is talking about or to clarify procedures that students are expected to complete.

Responses that are questions—Students' questions demonstrate that not knowing something is part of the learning process, even for students doing well in the content. Questions that will help everyone learn more provide diagnostic as well as shared learning opportunities.

Responses that are inappropriate or wrong—One consideration a teacher needs to make when responses are incorrect is whether the source is content- or language-oriented, or both. Some ELLs lack the linguistic competence to demonstrate their content knowledge and need support from the teacher. If the content is missing, the teacher can seize the moment to reteach or clarify misunderstandings.

Silent response—Teachers need to avoid a premature judgment that a silent student lacks ability or motivation to learn. An "I don't know" could actually mean "I don't know how" and requires a teacher to communicate belief in the student's ability to contribute to the discussion. Sometimes the teacher can engage the student by rephrasing the question. Other times, the teacher may just have to wait a little longer to get a response.

Figure 7.3. Response protocol. *Source*: Adapted from "Extending English-Language Learners' Classroom Interactions Using the Response Protocol," by K. A. J. Mohr & E. S. Mohr, 2007, *Reading Teacher, 60*, 440–450.

As Scarcella (2003) notes, "Among academics it is said:

If it stinks, it's biology.
If it blows up, it's chemistry.
If it doesn't work, it's physics.
If it's boring, it's English." (p. 91)

It is our hope that dynamic and responsive practices for English language learners in English classrooms make that old saw as outdated as Model Ts, high-button shoes, and low expectations for students like Arian, Abdurashid, and Raquel.

Note

1. This lesson was adapted from one written by Nancy Frey and Doug Fisher and is reprinted with permission from the National Association of Comics Art Educators.

References

Adger, C. T., Snow, C. E., & Christian, D. (Eds.). (2002). *What teachers need to know about language*. Washington, DC: Center for Applied Linguistics.

Afferbach, P., & Johnston, P. (1984). On the use of verbal reports in reading research. *Journal of Reading Behavior, 16*, 307–322.

Alfassi, M. (1998). Reading for meaning: The efficacy of reciprocal teaching in fostering reading comprehension in high school students in remedial reading classes. *American Educational Research Journal, 35*, 309–332.

Allen, J. (1999). *Words, words, words: Teaching vocabulary in grades 4–12*. York, ME: Stenhouse.

Anderson, R. C., & Pearson, P. D. (1984). A schema-theoretic view of basic processes in reading. In P. D. Pearson, R. Barr, M. L. Kamil, & P. Mosenthal (Eds.), *Handbook of reading research* (pp. 255–291). New York: Longman.

Andrews, R., Torgerson, C., Beverton, S., Freeman, A., Locke, T., Low, G., Robinson, A., & Zhu, D. (2006). The effect of grammar teaching on writing development. *British Educational Research Journal, 32*(1), 39–55.

Arnold, R. D. (1972). *A comparison of the neurological impress method, the language experience approach, and classroom teaching for children with reading disabilities* (Final report). Lafayette, IN: Purdue Research Foundation. (ERIC Document Reproduction Service No. ED 073428)

August, D., Carlo, M., Dressler, C., & Snow, C. (2005). The critical role of vocabulary development for English language learners. *Learning Disabilities Research and Practice, 20*(1), 50–57.

August, D., & Shanahan, T. (Eds.). (2006). *Developing literacy in second-language learners: Report of the National Literacy Panel on Language-Minority Children and Youth: Executive summary*. Mahwah, NJ: Erlbaum.

Basturkmen, H. (2002). Learner observation of, and reflection on, spoken discourse: An approach for teaching academic speaking. *TESOL Journal, 11*(2), 26–30.

Baumann, J. F., Edwards, E. C., Boland, E. M., Olejnik, S., & Kame'enui, E. J. (2003). Vocabulary tricks: Effects of instruction in morphology and context on fifth grade students' ability to derive and infer word meanings. *American Education Research Journal, 40*, 447–494.

Baumann, J. F., Kame'enui, E. J., & Ash, G. E. (2003). Research on vocabulary instruction: Voltaire redux. In J. Flood, D. Lapp, J. R. Squire, & J. M. Jensen (Eds.), *Handbook of research on teaching the English language arts* (2nd ed., pp. 752–785). Mahwah, NJ: Erlbaum.

Bean, J. C., Chappell, V. A., & Gillam, A. M. (2005). *Reading rhetorically: A reader for writers*. NewYork: Pearson/Longman.

Beck, I. L., McKeown, M. G., Hamilton, R. L., & Kucan, L. (1997). *Questioning the author: An approach for enhancing student engagement with text.* Newark, DE: International Reading Association.

Beck, I. L., McKeown, M. G., & Kucan, L. (2002). *Bringing words to life: Robust vocabulary instruction.* New York: Guilford Press.

Beck, I. L., Perfetti, C. A., & McKeown, M. G. (1982). The effects of long-term vocabulary instruction on lexical access and reading comprehension. *Journal of Educational Psychology, 74*, 506–521.

Becker, W. C. (1977). Teaching reading and language to the disadvantaged—What we have learned from field research. *Harvard Educational Review, 47*, 518–543.

Benrabah, M. (1997). Word stress—A source of unintelligibility in English. *International Review of Applied Linguistics in Language Teaching (IRAL) 35*, 157–165.

Biancarosa, G., & Snow, C. E. (2004). *Reading next—A vision for action and research in middle and high school literacy: A report to Carnegie Corporation of New York.* Washington, DC: Alliance for Excellent Education.

Blachowicz, C., & Fisher, P. J. (2002). *Teaching vocabulary in all classrooms* (2nd ed.). Upper Saddle River, NJ: Merrill/Prentice Hall.

Blachowicz, C. L. Z., & Fisher, P. (2000). Vocabulary instruction. In M. L. Kamil, P. B. Mosenthal, P. D. Pearson, & R. Barr (Eds.), *Handbook of Reading Research* (Vol. 3, pp. 503–523). Mahwah, NJ: Erlbaum.

Bliss, A. (2001). Rhetorical structures for multilingual and multicultural students. In C. G. Panetta (Ed.), *Contrastive rhetoric revisited and redefined* (pp. 15–30). Mahwah, NJ: Erlbaum.

Bloom, B. S., Englehart, M. D., Furst, E. J., Hill, W. H., & Krathwohl, D. R. (1956). *Taxonomy of educational objectives: The classification of educational goals. Handbook I: Cognitive domain.* New York: David McKay.

Boyle, O. F., & Peregoy, S. F. (1998). Literacy scaffolds: Strategies for first- and second-language readers and writers. In M. F. Optiz (Ed.), *Literacy instruction for culturally and linguistically diverse students* (pp. 150–157). Newark, DE: International Reading Association.

Brassell, D., & Flood, J. (2004). *Vocabulary strategies every teacher needs to know.* San Diego, CA: Academic Professional Development.

Buehl, D. (2005, September 27). *Scaffolding.* Retrieved November 4, 2006, from http://www.weac.org/News/2005-06/sept05/readingroomoct05.htm

Burgess, C. S. (1999). Speaking rate, fluency, and accentedness in monolingual English and bilingual Czech, French, and Japanese speakers. *Journal of the Acoustical Society of America, 106*, 2154.

Busching, B. A. (1981). Readers theatre: An education for language and life. *Language Arts, 58*, 330–338.

Campbell, L. R. (1996). Issues in service delivery to African American children. In A. G. Kamhi, K. E. Pollock, & J. L. Harris (Eds.), *Communication development and disorders in African American children: Research, assessment, and intervention* (pp. 73–94). Baltimore: Paul H. Brookes.

Capps, R., Fix, M., Murray, J., Ost, J., Passel, J. S., & Herwantoro, S. (2005). *The new demography of America's schools: Immigration and the no child left behind act.* Washington, DC: Urban Institute.

Carnine, L., & Carnine, D. (2004). The interaction of reading skills and science content knowledge when teaching struggling secondary students. *Reading and Writing Quarterly: Overcoming Learning Difficulties, 20,* 203–218.

Carr, K. S., Buchanan, D. L., Wentz, J. B., Weiss, M. L., & Brant, K. J. (2001). Not just for the primary grades: A bibliography of picture books for secondary content teachers. *Journal* of *Adolescent and Adult Literacy, 45,* 146–153.

Carrell, P. L. (1989). Metacognitive awareness and second language reading. *Modern Language Journal, 73,* 121–134.

Cazden, C. B. (1988). *Classroom discourse: The language of teaching and learning.* Portsmouth, NH: Heinemann.

Chall, J. S., Jacobs, V. A., & Baldwin, L. E. (1990). *The reading crisis: Why poor children fall behind.* Cambridge, MA: Harvard University Press.

Chamot, A. U., & O'Malley, J. M. (1996). The cognitive academic language learning approach: A model for linguistically diverse classrooms. *Elementary School Journal, 96,* 259–273.

Chela-Flores, B. (1994). On the acquisition of English rhythm: Theoretical and practical issues. *International Review of Applied Linguistics in Language Teaching (IRAL), 32,* 232–242.

Cisneros, S. (1991). *Woman hollering creek and other stories.* New York: Vintage.

Coady, J., Magoto, J. Hubbard, P., Graney, J., & Mokhtari, K. (1993). High frequency vocabulary and reading proficiency in ESL readers. In T. Huckin, M. Haynes, & J. Coady (Eds.), *Second language reading and vocabulary learning* (pp. 217–228). Norwood, NJ: Ablex.

Cobb, C. (2005). Literacy teams: Sharing leadership to improve student learning. *Reading Teacher, 58,* 472–474.

Connors, R. J. (2000). The erasure of the sentence. *College Composition and Communication, 52*(1), 96–128.

contrastive. (n.d.). *Dictionary.com Unabridged (v 1.1).* Retrieved November 4, 2006, from Dictionary.com website: http://dictionary.reference.com/browse/contrastive

Coxhead, A. (2000). A new academic word list. *TESOL Quarterly, 34,* 213–238.

Culham, R. (2003). *6 +1 traits of writing: The complete guide.* New York: Scholastic.

Cummins, J. (1979). Cognitive/academic language proficiency, linguistic interdependence, the optimum age question and some other matters. *Working Papers on Bilingualism, 19,* 121–129.

Cunningham, A. E., & Stanovich, K. E. (1998). What reading does for the mind. *American Educator, 2,* 8–15.

Danticat, E. (1994). *Breath, eyes, memory.* New York: Soho.

Davey, B. (1983). Think aloud: Modeling the cognitive processes of reading comprehension. *Journal of Reading, 27,* 44–47.

Davis, J. N. (1989). Facilitating effects of marginal glosses on foreign language reading. *Modern Language Journal, 73,* 41–48.

Davis, L. (1998). One hundred words. *TESOL Journal, 7*(6), 39.

De la Colina, M. G., Parker, R. I., Hasbrouck, J. E., & Lara-Alecio, R. (2001). Intensive intervention in reading fluency for at-risk beginning Spanish readers. *Bilingual Research Journal, 25,* 503–538.

Delpit, L. (1996). *Other people's children: Cultural conflict in the classroom.* New York: New Press.

Dessen, S. (2000). *Dreamland.* New York: Viking.

Doughty, C. (1991). Second language instruction does make a difference: Evidence from an empirical study of SL relativization. *Studies in Second Language Acquisition, 13,* 431–469.

Dowhower, S. L. (1994). Repeated reading revisited: Research into practice. *Reading and Writing Quarterly: Overcoming Learning Difficulties, 10, 343–358.*

Dubarry, M., & Alves de Lima, D. (2003, November 11). *Notes on generation 1.5.* Retrieved October 10, 2006, from De Anza College website: http://faculty.deanza.edu/alvesdelimadiana/stories/storyReader$438

Duke, N. K., & Pearson, P. D. (2002). Effective practices for developing reading comprehension. In A. E. Farstrup & S. J. Samuels (Eds.), *What research has to say about reading instruction* (3rd ed., pp. 205–242). Newark, DE: International Reading Association.

Dutro, S. (2005). Questions teachers are asking about courses of study for secondary English language learners. *California Reader, 39*(1), 45–58.

Dutro, S., & Moran, C. (2003). Rethinking English language instruction: An architectural approach. In G. G. Garcia (Ed.), *English learners: Reaching the highest level of English literacy* (pp. 227–258). Newark, DE: International Reading Association.

Eisner, W. (1985). *Comics and sequential art: Principles and practice of the world's most popular art form.* Tamarac, FL: Poorhouse Press.

Eisner, W. (1996). *Graphic storytelling and visual narrative.* Tamarac, FL: Poorhouse Press.

Elley, W. (1989). Vocabulary acquisition from listening to stories. *Reading Research Quarterly, 24,* 174–187.

Fearn, L., & Farnan, N. (2001). *Interactions: Teaching writing and the language arts.* Boston: Houghton Mifflin.

Feinberg, R. C. (2000). Newcomer schools: Salvation or segregated oblivion for immigrant students? *Theory into Practice, 39*(4), 220–227.

Feng, S., & Powers, K. (2005). The short- and long-term effect of explicit grammar instruction on fifth graders' writing. *Reading Improvement, 42*(2), 67–72.

Filmore, L., & Snow, C. (2000). *What teachers need to know about language.* Washington DC: Center for Applied Linguistics.

Fisher, D. (2004). Setting the "opportunity to read" standard: Resuscitating the SSR program in an urban high school. *Journal of Adolescent and Adult Literacy, 48*, 138–150.

Fisher, D., Flood, J., Lapp, D., & Frey, N. (2004). Interactive read-alouds: Is there a common set of implementation practices? *Reading Teacher, 58*, 8–17.

Fisher, D., & Frey, N. (2003). Writing instruction for struggling adolescent readers: A gradual release model. *Journal of Adolescent and Adult Literacy, 46*, 396–405.

Fisher, D., & Frey, N. (2004). *Improving adolescent literacy: Strategies at work.* Upper Saddle River, NJ: Merrill/Prentice Hall.

Fisher, D., Frey, N., Fearn, L., Farnan, N., & Petersen, F. (2004). Increasing writing achievement in an urban middle school. *Middle School Journal, 36*(2), 21–26.

Flood, J., Lapp, D., & Fisher, D. (2005). Neurological impress method plus. *Reading Psychology, 26*, 147–160.

Fox, H. (1994). *Listening to the world: Cultural issues in academic writing.* Urbana, IL: National Council of Teachers of English.

Freeman, Y. S., & Freeman, D. E. (with Mercuri, S.). (2002). *Closing the achievement gap: How to reach limited-formal-schooling and long-term English learners.* Portsmouth, NH: Heinemann.

Frey, N., & Fisher, D. (2006). *Language arts workshop: Purposeful reading and writing instruction.* Upper Saddle River, NJ: Merrill/Prentice Hall.

Frodesen, J., & Sasser, L. (2005). *Next generation writers: An emerging paradigm.* Presentation for the Pasadena Community College Mini-conference and Workshop, Pasadena, CA.

Fry, R. (2005). *The higher dropout rate of foreign-born teens: The role of schooling abroad.* Washington, DC: Pew Hispanic Center.

Fullan, M., Hill, P., & Crévola, C. (2006). *Breakthrough.* Thousand Oaks, CA: Corwin Press.

Gibbons, P. (2003, March 25). *Scaffolding academic language across the curriculum.* Paper presented at the annual meeting of the American Association for Applied Linguistics, Arlington, VA.

Graff, G., & Birkenstein, C. (2006). *"They say/I say": The moves that matter in academic writing*. New York: W. W. Norton.

Graham, S., & Perin, D. (2007). *Writing next: Effective strategies to improve writing of adolescents in middle and high schools—A report to Carnegie Corporation of New York*. Washington, DC: Alliance for Excellent Education.

Graves, M. F. (2006). *The vocabulary book: Learning and instruction*. New York: Teachers College Press.

Graves, M. F., & Watts-Taffe, S. M. (2002). The place of word consciousness in a research-based vocabulary program. In A. E. Farstrup & S. J. Samuels (Eds.), *What research has to say about reading instruction* (3rd ed., pp. 140–165). Newark, DE: International Reading Association.

Gribbin, B. (2005). Our ambivalence toward teaching grammar. *English Journal, 94*(3), 17–19.

Guterson, D. (1994). *Snow falling on cedars*. San Diego, CA: Harcourt Brace.

Hampton-Brown. (2002). *Language transfer issues for English learners*. Carmel, CA: Author.

Hart, B., & Risley, T. R. (1995). *Meaningful differences in the everyday experience of young American children*. Baltimore: Paul H. Brookes.

Hasbrouck, J. E., & Tindal, G. (1992). Curriculum-based oral reading fluency norms for students in grades 2 through 5. *Teaching Exceptional Children, 24*(3), 41–44.

Hatch, E., & Brown, C. (1995). *Vocabulary, semantics, and language education*. Cambridge, England: Cambridge University Press.

Heckelman, R. G. (1966). Using the neurological impress remedial reading method. *Academic Therapy, 1*, 235–239.

Heckelman, R. G. (1969). A neurological-impress method of remedial-reading instruction. *Academic Therapy, 4*, 277–282.

Herman, P.A. (1985). The effect of repeated readings on reading rate, speech pauses, and word recognition accuracy. *Reading Research Quarterly*, 20, 553–565.

Herman, P. A., Anderson, R. C., Pearson, P. D., & Nagy, W. E. (1987). Incidental acquisition of word meaning from expositions with varied text features. *Reading Research Quarterly, 22*, 263–284.

Herrell, A., & Jordan, M. (2003). *Fifty strategies for teaching English language learners* (2nd ed.). Upper Saddle River, NJ: Merrill/Prentice Hall.

Herrell, A. L. (2000). *Fifty strategies for teaching English language learners*. Upper Saddle River, NJ: Merrill/Prentice Hall.

Hesse, K. (1997). *Out of the dust*. New York: Scholastic.

Hill, J. D., & Flynn, K. M. (2006). *Classroom instruction that works with English language learners*. Alexandria, VA: Association for Supervision and Curriculum Development.

Hollingsworth, P. M. (1970). An experiment with the impress method of teaching reading. *Reading Teacher, 24,* 112–114.

Hosenfeld, C. (1977). A preliminary investigation of the reading strategies of successful and nonsuccessful second language learners. *System, 5,* 110–123.

Hudson, R. F., Lane, H. B., & Mercer, C. D. (2005). Writing prompts: The role of various priming conditions on the compositional fluency of developing writers. *Reading and Writing: An Interdisciplinary Journal, 18,* 473–495.

Hunt, I. (2002). *No promises in the wind.* New York: Berkley.

Hybels, S., & Weaver, R. L., II. (2000). *Communicating effectively* (6th ed.). New York: McGraw-Hill.

Indrasuta, C. (1988). Narrative styles in the writing of Thai and American students. In A. C. Purves (Ed.), *Writing across languages and cultures: Issues in contrastive rhetoric* (pp. 206–226). Beverly Hills, CA: Sage.

interact. (n.d.). *Roget's New Millennium Thesaurus, First Edition (v 1.3.1).* Retrieved February 2, 2007, from Thesaurus.com website: http://thesaurus.reference.com/browse/interact

interact. (n.d.). *WordNet 2.1.* Retrieved February 2, 2007, from Dictionary.com website: http://dictionary.reference.com/browse/interact

Ivey, G. (2002). Getting started: Manageable literacy practices. *Educational Leadership, 60*(3), 20–23.

Ivey, G. (2003). "The teacher makes it more explainable" and other reasons to read aloud in the intermediate grades. *Reading Teacher, 56,* 812–814.

Ivey, G., & Broaddus, K. (2001). "Just plain reading": A survey of what makes students want to read in middle school classrooms. *Reading Research Quarterly, 36,* 350–377.

Ivey, G., & Fisher, D. (2005). Learning from what doesn't work. *Educational Leadership, 63*(2), 8–14.

Ivey, G., & Fisher, D. (2006). *Creating literacy-rich schools for adolescents.* Alexandria, VA: Association for Supervision and Curriculum Development.

Jacobson, S., & Colón, E. (2006). *The 9/11 report: A graphic adaptation.* New York: Hill and Wang.

Jago, C. (2002). *Cohesive writing: Why concept is not enough.* Portsmouth, NH: Heinemann.

Jones, R. C., & Thomas, T. G. (2006). Leave no discipline behind. *Reading Teacher, 60,* 58–64.

Kaplan, R. (1966). Cultural thought patterns in inter-cultural education. *Language Learning, 16,* 1–20.

Kasper-Ferguson, S., & Moxley, R. A. (2002). Developing a writing package with student graphing of fluency. *Education and Treatment of Children, 25,* 249–267.

Keen, J. (2004). Sentence-combining and redrafting processes in the writing of secondary school students in the UK. *Linguistics and Education: An International Research Journal, 15*(1–2), 81–97.

Keene, E. O., & Zimmerman, S. (1997). *Mosaic of thought: Teaching comprehension in a reader's workshop.* Portsmouth, NH: Heinemann.

Kern, R. (2000). Notions of literacy. In *Literacy and language teaching* (pp. 13–41). New York: Oxford University Press.

Kindler, A. (2002). *Survey of the states' limited English proficient students and available educational programs and services, 2000–2001 summary report.* Washington, DC: National Clearinghouse for English Language Acquisition and Language Instruction Educational Programs. Retrieved October 15, 2006, from http://www.ncela.gwu.edu/expert/faq/05toplangs.html

Klare, G. R. (1984). Readability. In P. D. Pearson, R. Barr, M. L. Kamil, & P. Mosenthal (Eds.), *Handbook of reading research* (pp. 681–744). New York: Longman.

Knight, S. (1994). Dictionary: The tool of last resort in foreign language reading? A new perspective. *Modern Language Journal, 78,* 285–299.

Krashen, S. D. (1981). *Second language acquisition and second language learning.* New York: Pergamon Press.

Krashen, S. D. (1985). *The input hypothesis: Issues and implications.* New York: Longman.

Krashen, S. D. (1993). The case for free, voluntary reading. *Canadian Modern Language Review, 50*(1), 72–82.

Kucan, L., & Beck, I. L. (1997). Thinking aloud and reading comprehension research: Inquiry, instruction, and social interaction. *Review of Educational Research, 67,* 271–299.

Larsen-Freeman, D. (1997). Grammar and its teaching: Challenging the myths. *Eric Digest,* ED406829 97. Retrieved from http://www.ericdigests.org/1997-4/grammar.htm

Larsen-Freeman, D. (2000). *Techniques and principles in language teaching* (2nd ed.). Oxford, England: Oxford University Press.

Laufer, B., & Hadar, L. (1997). Assessing the effectiveness of monolingual, bilingual, and "bilingualised" dictionaries in the comprehension and production of new words. *Modern Language Journal, 81,* 189–196.

Leal, D. J. (2005). The word writing CAFE: Assessing student writing for complexity, accuracy, and fluency. *Reading Teacher, 59,* 340–350.

Leki, I. (1992). *Understanding ESL writers: A guide for teachers.* Portsmouth, NH: Heinemann.

LeMoine, N. (2006). *Standard English learners: Overlooked and underserved language minority students.* Presentation for California Association of Bilingual Education Annual Convention. San Jose, CA.

Levis, J. M. (1999). Intonation in theory and practice, revisited. *TESOL Quarterly, 33,* 37–63.

Lightbown, P. M. (1998). The importance of timing in focus on form. In C. Doughty & J. Williams (Eds.), *Focus on form in classroom second language acquisition* (pp. 177–196). Cambridge, England: Cambridge University Press.

Los Angeles Unified School District (LAUSD), Local District 5. (n.d.). *Academic English mastery and closing the achievement gap.* Retrieved October 20, 2006, from http://www.lausd.k12.ca.us/District_5/aemp.htm

Lucas, T. (2005). Language awareness and comprehension through puns among ESL learners. *Language Awareness, 14,* 221–238.

Malik, A. A. (1990). A psycholinguistic analysis of the reading behavior of EFL-proficient readers using culturally familiar and culturally nonfamiliar expository texts. *American Education Research Journal, 27,* 205–223.

Martin, D. (2004). *Language, literacy, and everything connected in between* [Power Point presentation]. Retrieved October 15, 2006, from http://www2.bc.edu/~guttenni/quest/docs/quest_literacy.pps

Martinez, M., Roser, N. L., & Strecker, S. (1998–1999). "I never thought I could be a star": A readers theatre ticket to fluency. *Reading Teacher, 52,* 326–334.

Marzano, R. J. (2004). *Building background knowledge for academic achievement: Research on what works in schools.* Alexandria, VA: Association for Supervision and Curriculum Development.

Marzano, R. J., & Pickering, D. J. (2005). *Building academic vocabulary: Teacher's manual.* Alexandria, VA: Association for Supervision and Curriculum Development.

Matthews, M. W., & Kesner, J. (2003). Children learning with peers: The confluence of peer status and literacy competence within small-group literacy events. *Reading Research Quarterly, 38,* 208–234.

McCauley, J. K., & McCauley, D. S. (1992). Using choral reading to promote language learning for ESL students. *Reading Teacher, 45,* 526–533.

Medoff, J. (2002). *Hunger point: A novel.* New York: Regan Books.

Mickle, S. F. (2001). *The turning hour.* Montgomery, AL: River City.

Mohr, K. A. J., & Mohr, E. S. (2007). Extending English-language learners' classroom interactions using the response protocol. *Reading Teacher, 60,* 440–450.

Morley, J. (1991). The pronunciation component in teaching English to speakers of other languages. *TESOL Quarterly, 25,* 481–520.

Munro, M. J., & Derwing, T. M. (1999). Foreign accent, comprehensibility, and intelligibility in the speech of second language learners. *Language Learning, 49,* 285–310.

Nagy, W. E., & Anderson, R. C. (1984). How many words are there in printed school English? *Reading Research Quarterly, 19,* 304–330.

Nagy, W. E., & Herman, P. A. (1984). *Limitations of vocabulary instruction* (Tech. Report No. 326). Urbana, IL: Center for the Study of Reading.

National Clearinghouse for English Language Acquisition and Language Instruction Educational Programs (NCELA). U.S. Department of Education. (2005). *The growing numbers of limited English proficient students, 1993/94–2003/04.* Retrieved October 7, 2006, from http://www.ncela.gwu.edu/policy/states/reports/statedata/2003LEP/GrowingLEP_0304_Dec05.pdf

National Council of Teachers of English, ELL Task Force. (2006). *Position paper on the role of English teachers in educating English language learners (ELLs).* Retrieved May 11, 2006, from http://www.ncte.org/about/over/positions/category/div/124545.htm

National Reading Panel. (2000). *Teaching children to read: An evidence-based assessment of the scientific research literature on reading and its implications for reading instruction: Reports of the subgroups* (NIH Publication No. 00-4754). Washington, DC: National Institute of Child Health and Human Development.

Nichols, J. N. (1980). Using paragraph frames to help remedial high school students with written assignments. *Journal of Reading, 24,* 228–231.

O'Brien, D. G., Stewart, R. A., & Moje, E. B. (1995). Why content literacy is difficult to infuse into the secondary school: Complexities of curriculum, pedagogy, and school culture. *Reading Research Quarterly, 30,* 442–463.

Oczkus, L. D. (2003). *Reciprocal teaching at work: Strategies for improving reading comprehension.* Newark, DE: International Reading Association.

Olshavsky, J. E. (1977). Reading as problem solving: An investigation of strategies. *Reading Research Quarterly, 12,* 654–674.

O'Malley, J. M., & Pierce, L. V. (1996). *Authentic assessment for English language learners: Practical approaches for teachers.* Reading, MA: Addison-Wesley.

Opitz, M. F., & Rasinski, T. V. (1998). *Good-bye round robin: 25 effective oral reading strategies.* Portsmouth, NH: Heinemann.

Palincsar, A. S. (1987). Reciprocal teaching: Can student discussion boost comprehension? *Instructor, 96*(5), 56–58, 60.

Palumbo, T. J., & Willcutt, J. R. (2006). Perspectives on fluency: English-language learners and students with dyslexia. In S. J. Samuels & A. E. Farstrup (Eds.), *What research has to say about fluency instruction* (pp. 159–178). Newark, DE: International Reading Association.

Paris, S. G., Lipson, M. Y., & Wixson, K. K. (1983). Becoming a strategic reader. *Contemporary Educational Psychology, 8,* 293–316.

Paris, S. G., Wasik, B. A., & Turner, J. C. (1991). The development of strategic readers. In R. Barr, M. L. Kamil, P. B. Mosenthal, & P. D. Pearson

(Eds.), *Handbook of Reading Research* (Vol. 2, pp. 609–640). New York: Longman.

Pearson, P. D., & Gallagher, M. C. (1983). The instruction of reading comprehension. *Contemporary Educational Psychology, 8*, 317–344.

Pendarvis, B., & Kneece, M. (2004). *The bristol board jungle.* New York: Nantier Beall Minoustchine.

Penno, J. F., Wilkinson, I. A. G., & Moore, D. W. (2002). Vocabulary acquisition from teacher explanation and repeated listening to stories: Do they overcome the Matthew effect? *Journal of Educational Psychology, 94*, 23–33.

Pew Hispanic Center. (2006, October). Foreign born at mid-decade: School enrollment by nativity: 2000 and 2005. In *A Statistical Portrait of the Hispanic and Foreign-Born Populations at Mid-Decade* (Table 21). Retrieved October 18, 2006, from http://pewhispanic.org/files/other/foreignborn/Table-21.pdf

Pilgreen, J., & Krashen, S. (1993). Sustained silent reading with English as a second language high school students: Impact on reading comprehension, reading frequency, and reading enjoyment. *School Library Media Quarterly, 22*, 21–23.

Portes, A., & Rumbaut, R. G. (2001). *Legacies: The story of the immigrant second generation.* Berkeley and New York: University of California Press and Russell Sage Foundation.

Portes, A., & Rumbaut, R.G. (2006). *Immigrant America: A portrait* (3rd ed.). Berkeley: University of California Press.

Raphael, T. E. (1984). Teaching learners about sources of information for answering comprehension questions. *Journal of Reading, 27*, 303–311.

Raphael, T. E. (1986). Teaching question-answer relationships, revisited. *Reading Teacher, 39*, 516–522.

Rasinski, T.V. (1990). Effects of repeated reading and listening-while-reading on reading fluency. *Journal of Educational Research, 83*, 147–150.

Rasinski, T. V. (2000). Speed does matter in reading. *Reading Teacher, 54*, 146–151.

Rasinski, T. V. (2004). Creating fluent readers. *Educational Leadership, 61*(6), 46–51.

Rasinski, T. V., & Padak, N. D. (2005). Fluency beyond the primary grades: Helping adolescent struggling readers. *Voices from the Middle, 13*(1), 34–41.

Rasinski, T. V., Padak, N. D., McKeon, C. A., Wilfong, L. G., Friedauer, J. A., & Heim, P. (2005). Is reading fluency a key for successful high school reading? *Journal of Adolescent and Adult Literacy, 49*, 22–27.

Reynolds, D. W. (2005). Linguistic correlates of second language literacy development: Evidence from middle-grade learner essays. *Journal of Second Language Writing, 14*(1), 19–45.

rhetoric. (n.d.). *Dictionary.com Unabridged (v 1.1)*. Retrieved November 4, 2006, from Dictionary.com website: http://dictionary.reference.com/browse/rhetoric

Richardson, J. S. (2000). *Read it aloud! Using literature in the secondary content classroom*. Newark, DE: International Reading Association.

Rickford, J. R. (1999). *African American vernacular English: Features, evolution, educational implications*. Malden, MA: Blackwell.

Rickford, J. R., & Rickford, A. A. (1995). Dialect readers revisited. *Linguistics and Education: An International Research Journal*, *7*(2), 107–128.

Robinson, W. S., & Tucker, S. (2005). *Texts and contexts: A contemporary approach to college writing* (6th ed.). Boston: Thomson Heinle.

Rothenberg, C., & Fisher, D. (2007). *Teaching English language learners: A differentiated approach*. Upper Saddle River, NJ: Pearson/Merrill/Prentice Hall.

Rumbaut, R. G., & Ima, K. (1988). *The adaptation of Southeast Asian refugee youth: A comparative study. Final report to the Office of Resettlement*. San Diego, CA: San Diego State University, Department of Sociology. (ERIC Document Reproduction Service No. ED299372)

Saddler, B. (2005). Sentence combining: A sentence-level writing intervention. *Reading Teacher, 58*, 468–471.

Saddler, B., & Graham, S. (2005). The effects of peer-assisted sentence-combining instruction on the writing performance of more and less skilled young writers. *Journal of Educational Psychology, 97*(1), 43–54.

Samuels, S. J. (2002). Reading fluency: Its development and assessment. In A. E. Farstrup & S. J. Samuels (Eds.), *What research has to say about reading instruction* (3rd ed., pp. 166–183). Newark, DE: International Reading Association.

Samway, K. D. (2006). *When English language learners write: Connecting research to practice, K–8*. Portsmouth, NH: Heinemann.

Scarcella, R., & Rumberger, R. W. (2000, Summer). Academic English key to long term success in school. *University of California Linguistic Minority Research Institute Newsletter, 9*, 1–2. Retrieved from http://lmri.ucsb.edu/publications/newsletters/v9n4.pdf

Scarcella, R. C. (2003). *Accelerating academic English: A focus on the English learner*. Oakland, CA: Regents of the University of California.

Schippert, P. (2005). Read alouds and vocabulary: A new way of teaching. *Illinois Reading Council Journal, 33*(3), 11–16.

Shafer, G., Swindle, S., & Joseph, N. (2003). What activity do you recommend for teaching grammar? *English Journal, 92*(3), 28–30.

Short, D., & Fitzsimmons, S. (2007). *Double the work: Challenges and solutions to acquiring language and academic literacy for adolescent English language learners—A report to Carnegie Corporation of New York*. Washington, DC: Alliance for Excellent Education.

Simons. H. D. (1971). Reading comprehension: The need for a new perspective. *Reading Research Quarterly, 6,* 338–363.

Smith, J. (1994). *Bone.* Columbus, OH: Cartoon Books.

Smith, W. (1981). The potential and problems of sentence combining. *English Journal,* 70(6), 79–81.

Snow, C. E. (2002). *Reading for understanding: Toward an R&D program in reading comprehension.* Santa Monica, CA: Rand.

Soanes, C., & Stevenson, A. (Eds.). (2006). *Concise Oxford English dictionary* (11th ed.). Oxford, England: Oxford University Press.

Söter, A. O. (1988). The second language learner and cultural transfer in narration. In A. C. Purves (Ed.), *Writing across languages and cultures: Issues in contrastive rhetoric* (pp. 177–205). Newbury Park, CA: Sage.

Spaulding, S., Carolino, B., & Amen, K. (2004). *Immigrant students and secondary school reform: Compendium of best practices* (K. B. Smith, Ed.). Washington, DC: Council of Chief State School Officers.

Spielberg, S. (Director). (1975). *Jaws.* [Motion picture]. United States: Universal Pictures.

Spinelli, J. (1990). *Maniac Magee.* Boston: Little, Brown.

Stahl, S. A. (1998). Four questions about vocabulary knowledge and reading and some answers. In C. R. Hynd (Ed.), *Learning from text across conceptual domains* (pp. 73–94). Mahwah, NJ: Erlbaum.

Steinbeck, J. (1939). *The grapes of wrath.* New York: Viking.

Sternberg, R. J. (1987). Most vocabulary is learned from context. In M. G. McKeown & M. E. Curtis (Eds.), *The nature of vocabulary acquisition* (pp. 89–105). Hillsdale, NJ: Erlbaum.

Tan, A. (1989). *The joy luck club.* New York: Putnam.

Terman, L. M. (1916). *The measurement of intelligence.* Boston: Houghton Mifflin.

Thorndike, E. L. (1917). Reading as reasoning: A study of mistakes in paragraph reading. *Journal of Educational Psychology, 8,* 323–332.

Trelease, J. (1993). *Read all about it! Great read-aloud stories, poems, and newspaper pieces for preteens and teens.* New York: Penguin.

Truss, L. (2004). *Eats, shoots and leaves: The zero tolerance approach to punctuation.* New York: Gotham Books.

Tyner, B., & Green, S. E. (2005). *Small-group reading instruction: A differentiated teaching model for intermediate readers, grades 3–8.* Newark, DE: International Reading Association.

Urbanski, C. D. (2005). *Using the workshop approach in the high school English classroom: Modeling effective writing, reading, and thinking strategies for student success.* Thousand Oaks, CA: Corwin Press.

Vacca, R. T., & Vacca, J. L. (1999). *Content area reading: Literacy and learning across the curriculum* (6th ed.). New York: Longman.

Vickers, C. H., & Ene, E. (2006). Grammatical accuracy and learner autonomy in advanced writing. *ELT Journal, 60,* 109–116.

Walqui, A. (2002). *Conceptual framework: Scaffolding instruction for English learners.* San Francisco: WestEd.

West, M. P. (1953). *A general service list of English words, with semantic frequencies and a supplementary word-list for the writing of popular science and technology.* London: Longmans, Green.

WestEd. (2002a). *Quality teaching for English learners.* Handout from Quality Teaching for English Learners (QTEL) Institute, July 2006. San Francisco: Author.

WestEd. (2002b). *Quality teaching for English learners: What makes reading difficult for adolescent English learners.* Handout from Quality Teaching for English Learners (QTEL) Institute, July 2006. San Francisco: Author.

WestEd. (2003a). *Scaffolding the development of literacy.* Handout from Quality Teaching for English Learners (QTEL) Institute, July 2006. San Francisco: Author.

WestEd. (2003b). *Teacher professional development.* Handout from Quality Teaching for English Learners (QTEL) Institute, July 2006. San Francisco: Author.

Wheeler, R. S., & Swords, R. (2006). *Code-switching: Teaching standard English in urban classrooms.* Urbana, IL: National Council of Teachers of English.

White, T. G., Graves, M. F., & Slater, W. H. (1990). Growth of reading vocabulary in diverse elementary schools: Decoding and word meaning. *Journal of Educational Psychology, 82,* 281–290.

White, T. G., Power, M. A., & White, S. (1989). Morphological analysis: Implications for teaching and understanding vocabulary growth. *Reading Research Quarterly, 24,* 283–304.

Wiesner, D. (1991). *Tuesday.* New York: Clarion Books.

World-Class Instructional Design and Assessment (WIDA) Consortium. (2004). *English language proficiency standards for English language learners in kindergarten through grade 12.* Retrieved October 20, 2006, from http://www.wida.us/Resources/standards/

Wright, J. G. (1893). First year English in the high school. *School Review, 1*(1), 15–23.

Wright, R. (1998). *Black boy.* New York: HarperCollins Perennial Classics.

Wright, R. (1998). *Haiku: This other world.* New York: Arcade.

Wu, S. (1996). Content-based ESL at the high school level: A case study. *Prospect, 11,* 18–36.

Wunder, J. R., Kaye, F. W., & Carstensen, V. (Eds.). (2001). *Americans view their dust bowl experience.* Boulder: University Press of Colorado.

Yule, G., & Macdonald, D. (1995). The different effects of pronunciation teaching. *International Review of Applied Linguistics in Language Teaching (IRAL), 33*, 345–350.

Zadina, J. (2004). *Brain research-based effective strategies to enhance learning and energize instruction.* Presentation for the U.S. Department of Education, Office of English Language Acquisition Summit. Washington, DC.

Zadina, J. (2005). *Brain research and instruction.* Presentation for the U.S. Department of Education, Office of English Language Acquisition Annual Summit. Washington, DC.

Zimmerman, C. (1997). Do reading and interactive vocabulary instruction make a difference? An empirical study. *TESOL Quarterly, 31*(1), 121–140.

Index

Authors

Douglas Fisher is professor of language and literacy education in the Department of Teacher Education at San Diego State University, the co-director for the Center for the Advancement of Reading at the California State University chancellor's office, and the past director of professional development for the City Heights Educational Collaborative. He is the recipient of the International Reading Association Celebrate Literacy Award, the Paul and Kate Farmer *English Journal* Writing Award for excellence in writing from the National Council of Teachers of English, as well as the Christa McAuliffe Award for Excellence in Teacher Education. He has published numerous articles on reading and literacy, differentiated instruction, and curriculum design as well as books, such as *Creating Literacy-rich Schools for Adolescents* (with Gay Ivey), *Improving Adolescent Literacy: Strategies at Work* (with Nancy Frey), and *Teaching English Language Learners: A Differentiated Approach* (with Carol Rothenberg). He has taught a variety of courses in SDSU's teacher-credentialing program as well as graduate-level courses on English language development and literacy. An early intervention specialist and language development specialist, he has taught high school English, writing, and literacy development to public school students. He can be reached at dfisher@mail.sdsu.edu.

Nancy Frey is associate professor of literacy in the School of Teacher Education at San Diego State University. She is a recipient of the Christa McAuliffe Award for Excellence in Teacher Education from the American Association of State Colleges and Universities. She has co-authored several books on literacy and was a co-recipient (with Doug Fisher) of NCTE's 2004 Kate and Paul Farmer *English Journal* Writing Award for outstanding writing for their article "Using Graphic Novels, Anime, and the Internet in an Urban High School," published in the *English Journal*. She teaches a variety of courses in elementary and secondary literacy in content area instruction and supporting students with diverse learning needs. She can be reached at nfrey@mail.sdsu.edu.

Carol Rothenberg is a staff developer in the area of literacy and English language learners. Providing support and guidance to both new and experienced teachers, she plans, coaches, and helps teachers reflect on instruction across the content areas and across the grade levels. She has worked with elementary and secondary schools throughout the San Diego Unified School District, training teachers and administrators on effective programs and instruction for English language learners. An experienced classroom teacher, Carol has taught English to adult migrant workers, bilingual special education, and Spanish. She currently designs and teaches classes for new teachers on effective instruction of English language learners. She can be reached at crothenberg@sandi.net.

Language Learners in the English Classroom: Readers' Discussion Guide

Chapter 1. The English Language Learner: "My Life's Path Is a Circle"

Preparing to Learn

Activating Background Knowledge

1. How has your school (district) been impacted by the numbers of English language learners?
2. What has your school (district) done to prepare teachers?
3. How has your own instruction (or instruction at your school/district) changed with the influx of English language learners?
4. What do you feel your strengths are in working with ELL students?
5. What do you feel you need to learn more about?

Building Background Knowledge

6. What are the demographics of your school's (district's) ELL students?
   - Numbers
   - Languages
   - Proficiency levels
   - Years of enrollment in U.S. schools
   - Prior education

Connecting to Personal Experience

7. What are the challenges that you notice your ELL students facing in your classroom?
8. How have you helped them face these challenges?

Chapter 2. Teaching and Learning in English: What Works

Preparing to Learn

1. Look at your state's ELA and ELD/ELP standards. How are they aligned? How are they different? (If your state does not have ELD/ELP standards, look at WIDA's [http://www.wida.us/standards/elp.aspx] or TESOL's [*PreK–12 English Language Proficiency Standards*. Alexandria, VA: Author, 2006].)

Interacting with Text

2. Analyze some ELL student writing samples. What evidence do you find of a lack of familiarity with the linguistic code, text structure, and/or rhetorical style that is different from errors you would expect to find in the writing of native English speakers?
3. Select one of the reports outlined in this chapter. Using a scale of 1 through 5 (5 = outstanding, consistent practice; 1 = not observed), rate yourself and your school on the implementation of the best practices listed. (Study groups—small groups or partners—each select a different report and share their findings with the whole group.)
4. What aspects of the gradual release of responsibility model are most visibly present in your instruction (your school)? Which are less so? Why? What do you need to fully implement this model?

Extending the Learning

5. Use the rating of your own instruction to draft an initial action plan.
6. Prioritize areas of need for your school and map out an initial action plan. (You will add to the individual and schoolwide plans as you continue reading and discussing this text.)

Chapter 3. Focus on Vocabulary: Getting the Just Right Word

Preparing to Learn

1. How do you select vocabulary to teach?
2. How do you teach it?
3. How do you assess learning?

Interacting with Text

4. Select a passage you are about to use with your students. What specialized vocabulary would you select to teach? What about general academic vocabulary? What affixes and roots might you teach? Are there any cognates? Plan a read-aloud: script your comments and questions; highlight focus vocabulary.
5. Examine your student writing samples. What mortar words do your students need to make their writing more comprehensible and cohesive?
6. What vocabulary strategy have you used successfully?

Extending the Learning

7. Try out your read-aloud with your students. How did it go? What worked? What would you do differently next time?
8. Observe a colleague conducting a read-aloud with his or her students. Hold a preobservation conference to discuss the purpose and the expected outcome. Hold a postobservation conference to discuss student learning. Share your experience in the study group.
9. Select a vocabulary strategy from the chapter to try with your students. Try it out and report back to the study group.
10. Identify actions you will take in your practice to build student vocabulary. Add to your individual action plan.
11. Discuss the schoolwide vocabulary learning approaches described in this chapter. Add one to your school action plan.

Chapter 4. Focus on Grammar: "It Is Blue?"

Preparing to Learn

1. Do you agree or disagree with the following statements? Why or why not?
   a. Grammar is acquired naturally; it need not be taught.
   b. Grammar structures are taught one at a time.
   c. A grammar text with repeated skill practice is the best way to teach grammar.
   d. I do not know enough about grammar to teach it.
2. Examine some student work samples. Select students at a few different proficiency levels, a couple of standard English learners, and a couple of native speakers of standard English. What do you notice about the types of grammatical errors they make?

Categorize the types of errors for each student. What commonalities do you notice among the students? What differences? Prioritize the errors and select one error type as an instructional focus for each student.

Interacting with Text

3. How might you use a contrastive rhetoric approach to teaching grammar?
4. Examine a piece of text you might use in your classroom. What opportunities does it offer to teach grammar at the subsentence level? At the sentence level? At the discourse level?
5. Using your student writing samples and your current unit of instruction, outline a short lesson that includes:
   a. Generative sentences
   b. Sentence combining
   c. Sentence syntax surgery

Extending the Learning

6. How can you incorporate these strategies into your daily or weekly instruction? Use your pacing guide, curriculum map, unit plan, or other framework.
7. What do English teachers need in order to provide effective grammar instruction?
8. What is the role of content area teachers in grammar instruction?
9. Add to your individual and schoolwide action plans.

Chapter 5. Focus on Fluency: More Than the Need for Speed

Preparing to Learn

1. What does fluency mean?
2. What opportunities do students in your classroom currently have to develop fluency?

Interacting with Text

3. Collect baseline data on your students. Time them three times for one minute each. Average their scores to determine:
   a. How many words per minute they can read. (Have students read aloud the same passage three times with a partner.)
   b. How many words per minute they can write.

4. How can you prepare students for oral presentations and speeches?
5. Select a writing genre you are currently working on with your students. Create a writing frame to support their writing.

Extending the Learning

6. Select one of the strategies described in the chapter and try it out with your students. How did it go? What did your students learn? What went well? What would you do differently next time?
7. How might content area teachers use these strategies in their classrooms to build students' fluency?
8. Add to your individual and schoolwide action plans.

Chapter 6. Focus on Comprehension: "The Cooperation of Many Forces"

Preparing to Learn

1. Read the following excerpt. Note the strategies you use to make meaning. What else would have helped your comprehension?

> One of the first demonstrations of the existence of major statistical regularities in language was carried out by the American philologist George Kingsley Zipf (1902–1950). His best known "law" proposes a constant relationship between the rank of a word in a frequency list, and the frequency with which it is used in a text.
>
> Factors such as efficiency and ease of communication appealed strongly to Zipf, who argued for a principle of "least effort" to explain the apparent equilibrium between diversity and uniformity in our use of sounds and words.
>
> Crystal, D. (1987). *The Cambridge Encyclopedia of Language* (p. 87). Melbourne, Australia: Cambridge University Press.

Interacting with Text

2. Which of the eight reading comprehension strategies identified by the National Reading Panel (2000) are a consistent element of your lessons? Which might need increased focus?
3. What types of questions do you most often ask your students? How do you ensure that all students participate?
4. How is small group instruction implemented in your classroom or school? What do teachers need in order to integrate it as a regular component of their instruction?

5. If you are reading this book as part of a study group: in groups of four, assign each member a role (predictor, questioner, clarifier, summarizer), select a paragraph or two, and practice the process of reciprocal teaching.
6. What do content area teachers need to know about reading comprehension?

Extending the Learning

7. Select an instructional focus and a piece of text you will use with your students. Then:
    a. Using Bloom's taxonomy, write a series of leveled questions designed to support comprehension.
    b. Design an advance organizer to build schema.
    c. Determine key elements of a think-aloud to model comprehension strategies.
8. Add to your individual and schoolwide action plans.

Chapter 7. The English Classroom: A Place for Language Learning

Preparing to Learn

1. Think of a skill you learned as a child. How did you learn it? What kind of "scaffolding" did you receive? How did you gain independence?

Interacting with Text

2. What are the similarities and differences in the instructional needs of your English language learners, standard English learners, and native speakers of standard English?
3. Think of a unit of study you recently taught. How did the instructional sequence prepare students to learn? How did students interact with text? What tasks helped to extend their learning?
4. Using this same unit of study, what did you do to gradually release responsibility for learning to the students—modeling, guided instruction, collaborative learning, independent work?

Extending the Learning

5. Select a unit of study you are about to teach. Review it to:
    a. Determine how it fits into the framework for instructional planning (Figure 7.1).

   b. Identify what, when, how, and for whom you can integrate vocabulary, grammar, fluency, and comprehension practice.

6. Review your individual and schoolwide action plans. Prioritize the actions and revise them.
7. Determine the first action you will take in your individual practice.
8. Determine the first action you will take as a school.

Teaching English Language Learners
Individual Action Plan

Area of Focus	Actions	Measurable Outcome	Timeline
Best Practice			
Vocabulary			
Grammar			
Fluency			
Comprehension			

Teaching English Language Learners
School Action Plan

Area of Focus	Persons Responsible	Actions	Timeline
Best Practice			
Vocabulary			
Grammar			
Fluency			
Comprehension			

This book was typeset in Palatino and Helvetica by Electronic Imaging.
Typefaces used on the cover were Champion HTF Welterweight
and Avenir Black Oblique.
The book was printed on 50-lb. Williamsburg Offset paper by Versa Press, Inc.